WALKING ON UIST
AND BARRA

About the Author

Mike Townsend's love of hills and wild places began when, as a teenager, he spent walking holidays in the Lake District and Snowdonia. Later, at Edinburgh University, his horizons expanded north to the Scottish Highlands, and he first glimpsed the Isles of Uist and Barra from the Cuillin of Skye back in 1969. Mike's interest in mountaineering at this time also took him further afield to the Alps and to Greenland.

 After graduating in geology, Mike was self-employed as a freelance mineralogist through much of the 1970s, which involved extensive travel and occasional mountaineering, principally in South America and Australasia.

 Mike moved to the Outer Hebrides in 1980 to work as a geography teacher on Barra, and relocated to Uist in 1988 to teach in Sgoil Lionacleit on the Isle of Benbecula. During this time, and indeed since his retirement in 2010, he has spent prolonged periods exploring the hills and coastline of the islands, particularly the more remote and unfrequented areas.

WALKING ON UIST AND BARRA

by Mike Townsend

JUNIPER HOUSE, MURLEY MOSS,
OXENHOLME ROAD, KENDAL, CUMBRIA LA9 7RL
www.cicerone.co.uk

© Mike Townsend 2012
Reprinted (with updates) 2015, 2018
ISBN: 978 1 85284 660 2

Printed by KHL Printing, Singapore

A catalogue record for this book is available from the British Library.
All photographs are by the author unless otherwise stated.

*This book is dedicated to the memory of my father, John Townsend,
who first introduced me to the Scottish mountains.*

*I to the hills will lift mine eyes,
from whence doth come mine aid.
My safety cometh from the Lord,
who heav'n and earth hath made.*
Scottish Psalter: Psalm 121 v 1-2

Front cover: Looking north from Eabhal, North Uist

CONTENTS

Route symbols on OS map extracts

route

variant

start point/finish point

variant finish

start/finish point

route direction

Features on the overview maps

National Scenic Areas

primary A roads

other A roads

ferry routes (with journey time)

For OS legend see OS maps.

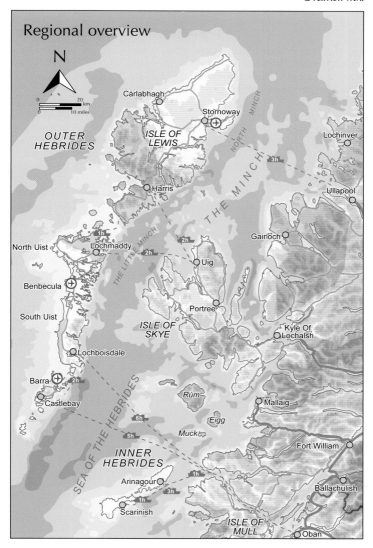

Regional overview

N

0   20 km
0   10 miles

OUTER
HEBRIDES

Càrlabhagh

ISLE OF
LEWIS

Stornoway

Lochinver

NORTH MINCH

THE MINCH

3h

Harris

Ullapool

THE LITTLE MINCH

North Uist

Lochmaddy

2h

2h

Gairloch

Uig

Benbecula

Portree

South Uist

ISLE OF
SKYE

Kyle Of
Lochalsh

Lochboisdale

Barra   2h

SEA OF THE HEBRIDES

Rùm

Castlebay

Eigg

Mallaig

6h

Muck

5h

INNER
HEBRIDES

Fort William

Arinagour

1h

Ballachulish

3h

Scarinish   1h

ISLE OF
MULL

Oban

Acknowledgements

This book would not have been written without the love and support of my wife, Peigi, and of our children, Maighread and Iain. I also wish to thank our friend Norman Maclean for his encouragement and advice. His anecdotes and good humour helped to keep the task in perspective.

I am grateful to the team at Cicerone for their guidance and direction and also to a large number of people, some of whom are listed, who provided helpful information: Alastair and Sarah Banks, Jamie Boyle, Mick Clout, Gwen Evans, Rhodri Evans, Johan Ferguson, Mary Galbraith, Margaret Gilfedder, Jonathan Grant, Bill Hart, Frank Horsman, Douglas and Sandra Hutton, Nick Ingledew, Stewart Johnson, David Kirk, Alick MacAulay, Alastair Macdonald, Alex Macdonald, George Macdonald, Hugh Macdonald, Iain Macdonald, Lachlan Macdonald, Neil Macdonald, Willie Macdonald, Alastair MacEachen, Mary Catherine MacIsaac, Sarah and John MacIsaac, Norman Macleod, Hector MacPherson, Roddy MacRury, Dorothy MacVicar, Martin Margulies, Angus and Anne Monk, Heather Moser, Brian Rabbitts, Malcolm Simpson, Walter Smith, Maggie Stewart, Sheena Stewart, Len Wilson, North Uist Medical Practice and Uist Outdoor Centre.

Finally, I wish to publicly acknowledge my gratitude to the people of Uist and Barra. I am privileged to call these islands my home.

Updates to this Guide

While every effort is made by our authors to ensure the accuracy of guidebooks as they go to print, changes can occur during the lifetime of an edition. Any updates that we know of for this guide will be on the Cicerone website (www.cicerone.co.uk/660/updates), so please check before planning your trip. We also advise that you check information about such things as transport, accommodation and shops locally. Even rights of way can be altered over time. We are always grateful for information about any discrepancies between a guidebook and the facts on the ground, sent by email to updates@cicerone.co.uk or by post to Cicerone, Juniper House, Murley Moss, Oxenholme Road, Kendal LA9 7RL.

Register your book: To sign up to receive free updates, special offers and GPX files where available, register your book at www.cicerone.co.uk.

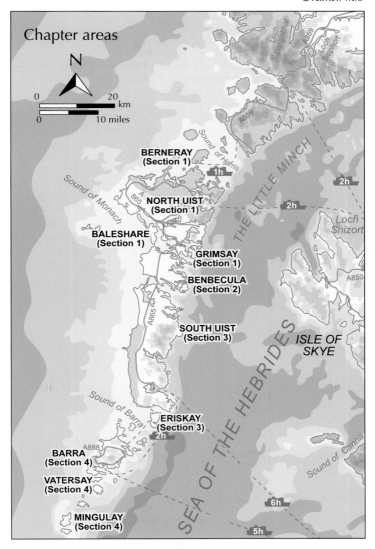

9

Sloc Rubha (Walk 1.11)

INTRODUCTION

The view north to Lì a Deas from Eabhal (Walk 1.8)

The islands south of the Sound of Harris in the Outer Hebridean archipelago are known collectively as the Uists and Barra. These islands lie on the very edge of Europe and the approach by air or sea serves to emphasise their awesome location and their sense of remoteness. Planes to Barra continue to land, improbably yet romantically, on the expanse of shell sand at Tràigh Mhòr, and on a clear, sunny day travellers to Benbecula are welcomed by aerial views of a wondrous landscape, a resplendent patchwork of water, rock and heather, fringed on the west by green machair and seemingly endless beaches of white sand. The sea journeys from Oban or from Uig in Skye are equally fascinating. As the ferry moves gradually westwards, each scan of the distant horizon reveals something fresh and intriguing as new islands slowly emerge from the grey-green Atlantic swell.

The islands themselves stretch over a distance of almost 100km between the two Bernerays: Berneray (Harris) in the north and the more southerly Berneray, the site of Barra

Head lighthouse, perched on a clifftop 200m above the ocean. In between are scores of other islands and islets with evocative names derived from their Gaelic and Norse heritage: Eriskay, Mingulay, Grimsay, Vatersay, Benbecula and Heisker. Today, only seven of the main islands are inhabited and these are linked by causeways: Berneray to Eriskay via North Uist, Benbecula and South Uist, and Barra to Vatersay. Others such as Mingulay have long been abandoned, adding to their atmosphere of mystery.

The physical landscape of these islands is extremely varied and offers superb walking country. The beaches, dunes and flat low-lying coastal machair generally found along the Atlantic shores contrast with the rugged, more mountainous areas in the east. Sea lochs penetrate far inland,

and the land itself contains myriad freshwater lochs and lochans.

The variation in physical landscape is reflected by diversity of wildlife habitat that is truly amazing, particularly across such a narrow east-west transect. In the upland areas surrounding Beinn Mhòr, Thacla and Eabhal red deer are frequently seen, and soaring eagles, golden and white-tailed, preside over this challenging, uncompromising terrain. At lower altitude, along the shores, grey seals are common, and otters may be seen on their daily migration between sea and fresh water. The machair is a breeding ground for thousands of waders, including dunlin and redshank, and the unique environmental conditions provide a refuge for the rare and elusive corncrake. In spring and summer this land, free from pollutants, is

Tràigh Eais on Barra's west coast (Walk 4.1)

clothed with an amazing assemblage of wild flowers: the vivid buttercups and dandelions growing alongside the more subtle hues of primroses and orchids.

Walking across this landscape, it is not only the physical scenery that captivates: history, too, is everywhere in evidence. You may come to these islands perhaps to retrace the footsteps of Bonnie Prince Charlie and Flora MacDonald, but wherever you walk, you become aware of humankind's attempts to survive, over thousands of years, in this environment. Not only are there duns, chambered cairns, standing stones and wheelhouses from the distant past, but also the scattered ruins of black houses and shielings from recent centuries – man's influence blending almost seamlessly with nature.

The natural environment also provides the basis for a range of leisure and sporting activities. In addition to the obvious attractions for the walker, there is scope for rock climbing on land and sea cliffs. The numerous lochs provide superb opportunities for trout fishing, and the clear, clean offshore waters and sheltered inlets along the east coast are ideal for diving and sea kayaking. Further west, the more exposed Atlantic is a challenging environment for surfers and windsurfers. At Aisgernis in South Uist, the rolling terrain of machair and dunes has produced a majestic links golf course.

Over the years these picturesque islands have had a high profile on both film and television. The classic film *Whisky Galore* was set on Barra, and more recent documentary programmes have enhanced the region's popularity as a holiday destination.

When should you visit the Uists and Barra? Undoubtedly, the months from April through to September are attractive on account of the kinder weather and almost limitless daylight. May and June are often particularly dry and sunny. Nevertheless, to visit these islands with sunshine and warmth as prerequisites is to ignore one of the main attractions. Whatever the weather, here is a place where you are truly close to raw nature with all its elements, a place where seasons appear to change rapidly, even in the space of a few hours. Throughout the year the vast skyscapes, almost devoid of human intervention, appear infinite and ever-changing, providing a canvas on which clouds and frequent rainbows paint a succession of matchless watercolours. In walking across this landscape, especially the hill country, you find genuine remoteness and solitude, so different from the teeming National Parks or the Munros with their processions of baggers.

Whatever time of year you choose to visit, you will be heartened by the warmth and friendliness of the people and will leave with enduring memories of a unique landscape and culture.

Banded gneiss on Beinn Mhòr, South Uist

GEOLOGY AND GEOMORPHOLOGY

The Uists and Barra are mainly composed of a metamorphic rock, Lewisian gneiss, which outcrops in many areas, particularly on the slopes of Eabhal and Lì a Tuath (Walks 1.8 and 1.5). Some of these rocks are dated at approximately 3 billion years old, making them among the oldest in Europe.

The gneiss has been repeatedly metamorphosed by high temperatures and intense pressure and is often banded and folded: clear evidence of its turbulent past. The rocks commonly contain a number of easily recognisable minerals: pink feldspar, white quartz and darker crystals, mainly hornblende and shiny biotite mica. East of Ruabhal in Benbecula (Walk 2.4), some outcrops also contain garnet, although the mineral surfaces have suffered from prolonged exposure to weathering.

In some places dykes of dolerite can be seen where molten rock has been forced up into the gneiss. The awesome cliff scenery of Mingulay (Walk 4.10) is, in part, attributable to the faster erosion of the softer, intrusive dykes compared with the harder, more resistant, gneiss. More recent igneous rocks are found on the Maddies: the stacks guarding the approach to Lochmaddy harbour. The rock is columnar basalt similar to that found on Skye.

The rocks have, over millions of years, been subjected to extensive

Marine erosion along a fault line

tectonic activity. The Hebridean Thrust runs along the eastern side of the islands, and the thrust zone itself is well exposed in Barra and South Uist, where there are outcrops of pseudotachylite, formed where rocks are thrust against each other. Faulting has been widespread throughout the region, and, as with the dykes, the shattered fault lines have been eroded and weathered faster than the surrounding rocks. Fault lines coincide with some of the most dramatic scenic features: the magnificent natural arches at Rubha Ghriminis (Walk 1.11) follow a line of tectonic disturbance, and also the long, narrow fjard (or shallow inlet) of Loch Euphort (Walk 1.8).

In the recent Ice Age, all of the islands were affected by glaciation to a certain extent, but the hills of South Uist in particular were sculpted by the erosive power of valley glaciers. Much of the underlying gneiss has been smoothed and scoured, and impressive corries were hewn from the northern slopes of Thacla and Beinn Mhòr. There is also a fine arête linking the two summits of Beinn Mhòr (Walk 3.6).

Glacial deposition was more widespread. There are extensive deposits of boulder clay, even on the smaller islands, and also some glacial erratics (boulders left by the retreating ice), some of which were transported many kilometres.

As one might expect in an island archipelago, the coastal scenery is both varied and dynamic. The cliffs and their dramatic stacks, caves and arches portray a gradual evolutionary process – the result of the incessant barrage of water against rock. However, the beaches, and their associated deposits of sand and shingle, are constantly changing. It is said that even within the last 200 years, the broad neck of sand, which forms part of the tombolo of northern Barra (Walk 4.1), was breached, before the gap was later closed again.

The island of Baleshare, off the west coast of North Uist (Walk 1.14), is also in a state of constant change, as longshore drift transports beach materials from the south to extend the spit at the northern end of the island. Sea level rises since the Ice Age have submerged areas close to the sea and helped to created the intricate coastline with its inlets and fjards. Historians claim that, in relatively recent times, a sand bridge connected Uist to Heisker, now 10km out in the Atlantic. The distinctive, white shell sand, which comprises a large proportion of the island beaches, is important, not only for its scenic quality. The accumulation of sand blowing inshore led to the formation of the machair, renowned for its unique habitat and wildlife.

HISTORY

The Uists and Barra provide a fascinating historical and archaeological record, with evidence dating back to the Neolithic era, 5000 years ago.

Standing stone on the South Uist moors

What makes these islands special is the way in which history so clearly permeates the local environment. The majority of the walks described pass monuments to times past: standing stones, chambered cairns, duns, wheelhouses and also the extensive ruins of more recently abandoned townships. The archaeological importance of the region is highlighted by the fact that, in recent years, excavations have been made on all the major islands.

The oldest significant site in the region, dating from Neolithic times, is Dùn Bharpa (Walk 4.3), a chambered burial cairn on Barra thought to be 5500 years old. At that time the area known as the machair, which occupies the western side of the islands, was formed from shell sand blown in from the Atlantic. Farming communities began to develop across this flat coastal plain. Further east, about 4500 years ago, the native woodland was replaced by peat and blanket bog as the climate became wetter.

Although this terrain was less hospitable for settlement, it is here that the oldest, major structures are found. The best-preserved sites are at Barpa Langais and Pobull Fhìnn on the slopes of Beinn Langais in North Uist (Walk 1.6) and are understood to be associated with the Beaker people whose characteristic pots have been unearthed. Barpa Langais is a chambered cairn thought to have been the scene of burnt burials. Sornach Coir' Fhìnn ('Fionn's people'), a stone

circle, is said to be named after Fionn mac Cumhaill, a Gaelic hero. Eilean Dòmhnuill, an islet in Loch Olabhat in North Uist, is believed to be Scotland's oldest example of a crannog, an artificial island used for settlement. Radio carbon dating suggests that this site was originally inhabited prior to 2500BC.

Moving forward to the Bronze Age, important recent discoveries have been made. Sheffield University's extraordinary excavation at Cladh Hàlainn (Walk 3.12) in South Uist is the only British site where prehistoric mummies have been found. The mummies, contemporaneous with Egyptian king Tutankhamun, had been preserved in peat at least a century before burial. At Allathasdal (Walk 4.3), on the west side of Barra, Channel 4's *Time Team* made a detailed study of a Bronze Age cemetery exposed by erosion of the sand dunes in 2005. The importance of this discovery, which also includes Iron Age houses, is said to be comparable with the well-known site at Skara Brae in Orkney.

The evidence of Iron Age settlement in the region is much more extensive, with a large number of duns and wheelhouses scattered throughout the islands. A dun is a stone-built fortified settlement and almost a hundred duns have been located on North Uist alone, many of them marked on OS maps. Most of these seem to have been originally built for defensive purposes.

Some, such as Dùn Sgùrabhal (Walk 4.1) on Barra, were built on hilltops, whereas others were located on islets or promontories. Access to the islets is generally by causeways, but often constructed from submerged stones, with gaps and sharp turns to deter potential intruders. The larger duns, such as Dùn an Sticir near Newton and Dùn Bàn on Barra, which have a more elaborate form of construction, are officially classed as brochs.

Wheelhouses, or aisled round-houses as they are sometimes known, have been discovered in various locations, but most have now fallen into decay, like the site at Kilpheder in South Uist. The wheelhouse in Grimsay (Walk 1.10) remains a fine example.

The Norse domination of the islands lasted for almost four centuries from AD900 to AD1200. The Hebridean islands were used as stopping off points on Viking forays to England and Ireland, but there were also some permanent settlements, particularly in South Uist where a Norse farm was recently uncovered. A Viking fort was excavated at Udal in North Uist (Walk 1.2) in the 1960s. The extensive Norse influence has been passed down to the present through many of the local place names such as Vatersay ('island of water') and Langais ('long ridge'), and also through surnames such as MacAskill ('son of Askell').

Following on from the Norse period, between 1336 and 1493, the Western Isles fell under the authority

The Grimsay Wheelhouse (Walk 1.10)

Caisteal Chiosmuil, Isle of Barra

of the Lord of the Isles. John of Islay and his successors were able to rule this sea-bound region by use of naval power, with fleets of galleys (*birlinn*) to subdue any opposition. The Trinity Temple (Teampull na Trianaid) at Carinish in North Uist, the scene of recent restoration work, dates from the 13th century and is believed to have been rebuilt in the 14th century by Christina, aunt of Amy MacRuari who was married to John, the first Lord of the Isles. Borgh Castle (Caisteal Bhuirgh) in Benbecula (Walk 2.1) was also built at this time.

Caisteal Chiosmuil, in its stunning position on a rocky islet in Bàgh a' Chaisteil on Barra, dates from the 15th century (or possibly earlier) and

was the stronghold of the MacNeils. The power and influence of the head of the clan MacNeil was considerable. It was said that after the clan chief had finished his meal, heralds would be dispatched to make loud the proclamation: 'Ye Kings, Princes, and Potentates of all the earth, be it known unto you that MacNeil of Barra has dined; the rest of the world may dine now.' One of the MacNeils, Ruari the Turbulent, was renowned for his acts of piracy, and the castle became a treasure trove of Spanish sherry and English gold. Caisteal Chiosmuil, along with the whole island of Barra, was sold by the MacNeils in the 19th century to pay off debts. However, the Castle was bought back by a

19

descendant in 1937 and has since been restored. It is now in the care of Historic Scotland.

The earliest evidence of Christian influence is found on Barra: the churchyard at Cille Bharra (Walk 4.1) is believed to date from the 9th century. An interesting artefact found there was a Christian-Nordic runic stone. Dating from the 10th century, it had a Celtic cross on one side with a runic inscription on the other. Some names from the Norse period suggest a monastic presence in the region: Pabbay, for instance, is derived from *papa ey*: 'the monk's isle'. At Tobha Mòr in South Uist (Walk 3.11) there is an impressive site comprising a number of ruined churches and chapels. The oldest of these is Teampull Mòr, St Mary's, built in the 13th century. Nunton House at Baile nan Cailleach

in Benbecula is believed to have been a nunnery back in the 14th century. Nearby is an old chapel and grave-yard (Walk 2.2).

Following the declining influence of the Lord of the Isles at the end of the 15th century, Clanranald assumed the principal position of power and authority in Benbecula and South Uist. It was Allan MacDonald, chief of Clanranald, who built Ormiclate Castle in South Uist. The castle took seven years to build, from 1701 to 1708, but was only occupied for seven more! The story goes that on the same day as the Battle of Sheriffmuir in 1715, a side of venison caught fire in the castle kitchen. The castle was destroyed, and was never rebuilt. The ruins remain impressive to this day, but are now in a dangerous state of disrepair.

Burial ground with St Mary's Chapel (Walk 2.2)

No account of the history of the area, however brief, would be complete without mention of Prince Charles Edward Stuart – Bonnie Prince Charlie. The Prince made two visits to these islands. He first came ashore on Eriskay in 1745, on his way to Glenfinnan, no doubt with high hopes of victory. However, his second visit, the following year, was while escaping after the Battle of Culloden. He found refuge in South Uist and Benbecula before sailing to Skye, aided by Flora MacDonald, a native of South Uist. The sea crossing from Ròisinis (Walk 2.3) to 'The Misty Isle' is recounted in the Skye Boat Song.

Moving forward to more recent times, the 19th century was a period of great depopulation caused by migration, both voluntary and forced. Hardship and overcrowding at home, and the hope of a better life elsewhere, caused many to leave voluntarily. However, during the Clearances, thousands of people were forcibly removed from their homes as areas of fertile land were taken over for sheep. Many were forced to emigrate to Canada and Australia, and those who remained were relocated to unfamiliar, hostile surroundings. People cleared from Solas tried without success to establish a permanent settlement at Brèinis on the north side of Loch Euphort. Evidence of this tragic era is seen in many places, and widespread ruins testify to once flourishing communities.

These islands suffered huge losses during both World Wars, but those who did return after the First World War faced a difficult homecoming. Promised 'a land fit for heroes', many were in reality both landless and unemployed. In their desperation, men in some areas were driven to raid the land, moving the cattle out and then ploughing the soil. Some were arrested and subsequently jailed in Inverness. However, their plight was finally acknowledged. The land was divided into smallholdings, which remain to this day.

PLANTS AND WILDLIFE

The Uists and Barra contain a remarkable range of habitats for such a small area: upland, moorland, wetland, loch, machair and coastal, sandy and rocky. Within the space of a few kilometres one can travel from sand dunes and coastal machair, with their alkaline, calcareous soils, to the blanket bogs and acidic soils of the uplands and heather moorland.

Despite the absence of trees on the islands, various plants – wild flowers in particular – are found in great abundance and diversity. The marshy areas on the east side of the Uists support an assortment of water-loving plants such as bog cotton and the insectivorous species, sundew and butterwort. However, it is on the machair that the flora occupies centre stage. The Uists are almost unique in providing a cultivated machair

Relaxing peacefully on the machair

where organic fertiliser, mainly seaweed, is applied to the arable land. The result, in the springtime and early summer, is truly memorable: a dense infusion of colours stretching across the coastal plain. Although the individual species, such as red clover, wild pansies and bird's foot trefoil, are

Primroses flourish in sheltered ravines

◀ *The Northern Marsh Orchid*

widespread and well known, it is the interplay of colours that delights the eye. In the northern part of Barra near Eòlaigearraidh and also on Vatersay, where only cattle are grazed, springtime unveils a subtle, pale yellow carpet of primroses.

As well as the more common plants and flowers, there are rarer species to provide additional interest: the Hebridean Marsh Orchid, endemic to North Uist, and also the Irish Lady's-tresses Orchid, recently identified in Benbecula. The island of Eriskay is home to the Prince's flower, Sea Bindweed, reputedly brought ashore by Bonnie Prince Charlie.

The different habitats support a range of contrasting creatures, both great and small. The wild flowers of the machair provide nectar for the great yellow bumblebee and, in autumn, the moorland areas are a refuge for thousands of hairy caterpillars, 'woolly bears', larvae of the garden tiger moth. The islands of North Uist, South Uist and Benbecula have large red deer populations and, although greater numbers are seen on the hills, stags and hinds are often seen by the roadside, particularly at dawn and dusk.

The vast areas of water, both fresh and sea, support a variety of fish and mammals. The lochs of the Uists are renowned for their brown trout. Seals are common around the shores, and Heisker, 12km west of Benbecula, is the site of the world's second largest breeding colony of grey seals. Otters are also relatively common and sometimes seen moving between loch and shore, but they are more elusive. However, otter spotting walks are

Mute swans on Loch Bì, South Uist

arranged locally, and these provide a good chance of a sighting (Walk 1.6). In offshore waters there are bottle-nosed dolphins, most easily seen from the inter-island ferries.

The range of bird species is extensive, and many may be sighted from the roadside, even without the aid of binoculars. In the mountains and across the moorlands there are numerous birds of prey, including golden eagle, white-tailed eagle, hen harrier, buzzard, merlin, peregrine and the short-eared owl. In recent years the RSPB warden in North Uist has established a 'Golden Eagle Watch' to enable the public to observe the nesting birds (contact Jamie Boyle on 0776 8042547). The white-tailed eagle, surprisingly, may often be sighted in the vicinity of the Lochmaddy ferry terminal.

The machair is also an important ornithological environment and is one of the remaining strongholds of the corncrake, whose rasping summer calls rival the sound of multitudes of greylag geese. There are also a variety of waders such as lapwing, dunlin, oystercatcher, redshank and ringed plover. The freshwater lochs draw seasonal visitors: in winter, whooper swans, particularly on Loch Bì in South Uist, and in summer, the red-necked phalarope on Loch Mòr in Benbecula.

Along the coasts, too, there is great variety. In addition to the fulmars, gulls and terns commonly seen, you could catch sight of puffins,

razorbills, guillemots and great skua on Mingulay.

For keen ornithologists, the Uists and Barra provide opportunities to see rare visitors normally found only in other geographical regions. Individual snowy owls return, most years, to the machair area north of Solas in North Uist. In the year 2000, rare visitors arrived from two different continents: from Asia the long-tailed shrike, and from North America the hooded merganser. Futher details are available from Brian Rabbitts, tel. 01876 580328.

TRANSPORT

To the islands

Transport to the Uists and Barra is by air or ferry. Flights go daily between Glasgow and Benbecula, and on weekdays to Barra where they land on a tidal beach, the only regular commercial flight to do so anywhere in the world. There are also regular flights beween Stornoway and Benbecula with a connecting flight to Barra. Air transport is operated by Flybe. Details of timetable and prices are available at www.flybe.com.

The main ferries to the islands leave from Oban and from Uig in Skye, and are operated by Caledonian MacBrayne (www.calmac.co.uk). Travelling from the south, your choice will depend partly on your destination, but also on whether you prefer a shorter drive and longer sailing, or vice versa. The Oban route goes to

The ferry arrives at Lochmaddy

Castlebay on Barra and Lochboisdale in South Uist, taking approximately 5hrs direct. The Uig option takes you to Lochmaddy in North Uist with a journey time of under 2hrs. Both ferries are vehicular and have an efficient roll-on/roll-off facility. In summer the sailings are almost daily on both routes, but from October to April journeys are less frequent. It is important to check sailing times and, in peak season, to book vehicles well in advance. The introduction of cheaper RET (Road Equivalent Tariff) fares in recent years was accompanied by a marked increase in advance bookings.

Caledonian MacBrayne run frequent inter-island connections from Harris to Berneray, and also between Barra and Eriskay. However, as with the mainland ferries, it is advisable to book in advance. There are numerous options available. If your intention is to travel north or south visiting a number of islands, it might be worth buying an Island Hopscotch ticket.

Within the islands
There is a regular bus service running right through the Uists from Berneray to Eriskay, and this connects with the inter-island ferry services. However, access to the more isolated areas is more difficult and the bus only stops for passengers at some road ends. A local bus service also runs around the Barra circular, with connecting branches to the airport and Eriskay ferry link. Details of bus timetables and connections may be obtained on

A causeway, not just for cars

the Comhairle nan Eilean Siar website (www.cne-siar.gov.uk).

Car hire is available from a number of garages (see Appendix D), and they will deliver vehicles to the airports or ferry terminals on request. Bicycles can also be hired on Barra, North Uist and South Uist. Details are in Appendix D.

Driving on the islands is sometimes challenging, particularly for those unfamiliar with single-track roads. The passing places are obviously needed to allow oncoming traffic to proceed, but are also useful to enable faster traffic to overtake.

It is wise to travel at a moderate pace, partly because of the many blind bends and summits, but also to be prepared for a number of animals that frequently stray, or even sunbathe, on the roads. Sheep are the obvious culprit, and are especially dangerous in the early summer when lambs frequently make an unpredictable dash to join their mothers. Deer are also relatively common in the Uists, particularly at dawn and dusk. As the causeway signs suggest, you may also see otters crossing the roads.

ACCOMMODATION AND FACILITIES

The islands offer a range of accommodation to suit different tastes and budgets: hotels, guesthouses, bed and breakfasts, self-catering, hostels, bunkhouses and also serviced sites for tents, caravans and motorhomes.

Details of accommodation are available from the tourist information offices in Castlebay, Lochboisdale and Lochmaddy, which are open from April to October (www.visithebrides.com/tic). It is important to book well ahead, particularly in the summer months. Hotels and bed and breakfasts on Barra are quickly filled at peak times such as Fèis Bharraigh, a festival of Gaelic music and drama held annually in early July.

There are cafés and other places for food and refreshment across all the major islands (see Appendix D).

Most shops, banks, and additional services are found in the main villages: Castlebay (Barra), Lochboisdale and Daliburgh (South Uist), Balivanich (Benbecula) and Lochmaddy (North Uist). Details of these services are also given in Appendix D.

SAFETY

When walking over hills and along coastlines, safety is a major consideration. It is essential to take care close to obvious dangers such as land and sea cliffs, but on some of the islands there are also hidden, more subtle hazards such as marsh or sinking sand, which may look harmless to the casual observer. Furthermore, the extensive intertidal beaches and salt flats with their gentle gradients are quickly inundated as the tide rushes in.

The routes described in this guide, apart from Eabhal from Loch Euphort (Walk 1.8), are not actually tide dependent, but the beach walks are probably more enjoyable when the sands are exposed at low tide. It is important to check the tides, both in the interests of safety and to ensure that the chosen route is accessible.

The weather on the islands may be unpredictable

Walking is for all ages, but only with the right footwear

Details are available from tourist information offices (Appendix D).

The absence of paths and markers over many of the hills highlights the importance of sound navigational skills, and a map and compass, or GPS, should always be on hand. Routes may appear relatively obvious and straightforward in clear weather, but in mist the landscape quickly becomes unfamiliar and deceptive. It is advisable to have at least two people in a party, and it is vital to leave a detailed route plan and time schedule with someone in case of mishap or delay. A mobile phone is useful, but not always reliable in some areas. Depending on the provider, there are certain blind spots where a signal may, at best, be faint or intermittent. However, emergency cover should always be available by calling 999.

The most suitable footwear and clothing will depend on the route, but almost all the walks across hill country or moorland require good walking boots and gaiters to keep feet dry. A waterproof, windproof jacket and trousers along with a warm hat and gloves are essential, even when the weather appears favourable. Conditions may deteriorate rapidly and it is often difficult to find shelter on the exposed hillsides. A torch, whistle, first aid kit, survival bag and emergency supplies of food and water are also important requirements for the longer outings. The beach walks provide very different conditions. On a sunny or partially cloudy day at any time of year, the water and white sand reflect solar radiation and may quickly cause sunburn. Wear a high-factor sun block for protection.

The Beinn Mhòr ridge in winter (photo: D Kirk)

Before setting out, check a detailed weather forecast. The shipping forecasts on BBC Radio 4 provide accurate information on wind speed and visibility for the neighbouring offshore areas Hebrides and Minches.

There are two wee beasties, which, although not really a safety concern, may still cause serious discomfort. Although not as widespread as on neighbouring islands such as Skye and Rùm, the midge may sometimes be an unwelcome companion. Chemists and internet suppliers now provide a wide range of deterrents with a variety of fragrances, but in extremis fine mesh apparel is probably the only truly effective protection. It is better to arrive prepared!

Another small parasite, arguably more harmful than the midge, is the tick, which unfortunately has an appetite for human blood. Ticks may attach themselves to the skin as you walk through long grass or heather, but only later, as the site of the tick bite begins to itch, is their presence apparent. Ticks should be removed using tweezers or a special instrument obtainable from the local pharmacy (tel. 01876 500333). On rare occasions, ticks may transmit Lyme disease. If the site of a tick bite becomes inflamed, seek medical advice. To reduce the risk of tick bites it is wise to cover the skin – wear long trousers and long-sleeved shirts.

The walks described in this guide are suggested routes, based on good walking conditions, and are not necessarily definitive. Use personal judgement to modify precise directions according to the tide or the weather, and for safety purposes. For example, there may be a gale blowing, making Beinn Mhòr's summit arête unacceptably hazardous, or there may be an unexpected bull in a nearby field.

ACCESS

Following the Land Reform (Scotland) Act of 2003, walking access should, in theory, be possible in almost all areas of the Uists and Barra. At the same time, walkers should adhere to the three key principles of the Scottish Outdoor Access Code: to respect the interests of other people, to take responsibility for one's own actions and to care for the environment. Full details are on the Scottish National Heritage website (www.snh.org.uk).

In reality, much of the land is criss-crossed by barbed wire fences. This can make direct access to certain sites problematical, and also makes straight-line navigation in some areas well nigh impossible. The walks in this guide have been specifically chosen to follow existing paths when available, and to target gates and stiles for crossing fences.

There are a number of specific access issues:

- Dogs must be kept under control at all times, but especially during the lambing season.
- In the months of June and July, particular care must be taken when walking near nesting sites.
- In spring and summer, please avoid walking on cultivated land.
- To avoid encountering stalking parties in the shooting season (principally October to December), it is advisable to contact North Uist Estate (tel. 01876 500329), or Stòras Uibhist (tel. 01878 700101).
- The Armed Forces are sometimes active in the area, particularly

The path up Ruabhal (Walk 2.4)

along the northern section of the Machair Way. Red flags warn of potential danger. To check access, contact the Range Controller (tel. 01870 604449).

Wild camping is also possible and there are many excellent sites, but it is wise to avoid drinking water from stagnant pools. When leaving a site, ensure you leave no trace. Despite the absence of trees on the islands, fires may spread very quickly across the moors, and are difficult to contain; it is vital to ensure that campfires are safely extinguished.

USING THE GUIDE

The routes in this book have been chosen not only to give walks of different length, but also to reflect the contrasting environments and habitats that exist on these islands. There are several walks into the wilder, more mountainous areas, and these tend to be longer and more serious outings requiring walking experience and navigational awareness. However, some smaller hills such as Ruabhal (Walk 2.4) have also been included to allow the moorland habitat to be sampled relatively easily.

The different routes offer a taste of the stark variations in coastline. There are a number of splendid beach excursions, but also clifftop walks, taking full advantage of the spectacular caves, stacks and arches.

The routes are divided into four sections to cover each of the main islands: North Uist, Benbecula, South Uist and Barra. The smaller isles – Baleshare, Berneray, Eriskay, Grimsay, Mingulay and Vatersay – are included in whichever of these sections is logistically the most convenient. All of the islands are readily accessible, apart from Mingulay, which requires a boat hire from Castlebay (contact Barra Fishing Charters on 01871 890384).

Each route description provides information on starting and finishing points. For linear routes guidance is given on how to access both the start and end locations. Distance and Total Ascent are given, as well as approximate walking times based on an average level of fitness. Route times may appear long for relatively short distances on the map. However, walking across trackless moorland is often strenuous and surprisingly time-consuming. The Total Ascent includes the combined height climbed on both the outward and return journeys.

Small 1:50,000 OS map extracts accompany the route descriptions, but it is essential to carry the complete maps either at 1:50,000 or 1:25,000 scale. These maps not only set the route in context, but also provide coverage of the surrounding area in case of navigational problems. Where a feature is referred to in a route description which is marked only on the 1:25,000 map, and therefore not on the map extract in this guide, 'Explorer map' appears in brackets after the reference. The 1:50,000 Landranger maps relevant to the region are Sheets

Road signs on the islands are in both Gaelic and English

Baile nan Cailleach
Nunton

18, 22 and 31. The 1:25,000 Explorer Sheets 452, 453 and 454 cover the area in more detail. The place names used in the route descriptions are the Gaelic names seen on the OS maps. Both English and Gaelic names for the different islands are used in the section headings.

A summary of the routes is provided in Appendix B.

Language and place names

The Isles of Uist and Barra remain one of the few areas in Scotland where the Gaelic language is widely used. Although the number of fluent speakers has undoubtedly declined in recent years, the 2001 census recorded that within the Outer Hebrides almost 60 per cent of the population were Gaelic speakers.

Visitors to these islands will notice that the road signs are in Gaelic and English, and the OS maps now use Gaelic spellings, or Gaelic options, for almost all place names. Some words may appear vaguely familiar, particularly to visitors from Ireland or Wales, where the native languages are related to Scottish Gaelic. Learning the language is an interesting challenge. You might start by asking the way to your destination using the Gaelic name.

Many of the place names in Uist and Barra are derived from Norse and Gaelic roots. Some owe their origins to characters renowned in their day: Berneray and Eriskay are from the Norse, meaning 'Bjorn's island' and 'Eric's island'. Many places were named in regard to the physical landscape: for instance, Brevig (Brèibhig) on Barra from the Norse meaning 'broad bay' and Am Bàgh Mòr from the Gaelic for 'big bay'. A glossary of words and suffixes commonly found on the maps is provided in Appendix A.

1 NORTH UIST
Uibhist a Tuath

Cliffs near Hosta (Walk 1.12)

INTRODUCTION

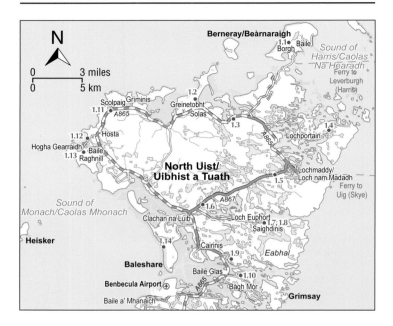

North Uist is an extraordinary island: almost half of it is covered by water. The combination of freshwater and sea loch occupies large swathes of the landscape and creates a seemingly impassable barrier to the walker.

The routes here have been chosen to provide the walker with memorable experiences of this unique landscape. A balance has been struck between the more isolated hill country of the east and the varied coastal scenery and habitats found further west.

Two main roads, the A865 and A867, combine to provide a circular route around the island, although these roads are single track for much of the way. The principal secondary roads are the B894 from Clachan na Luib to Loch Euphort and the B893 heading north to Berneray. The main settlement for North Uist is in Lochmaddy, also the terminal for the ferry from Uig in Skye.

WALK 1.1
Berneray (Beàrnaraigh)

Start/Finish	The car park beside Berneray Community Hall (NF 909 813)
Distance	12km
Total Ascent	200m
Time	5–6hrs
Terrain	Machair and sandy coast
Maps	OS Explorer 454; OS Landranger 18

Berneray, an island off the north coast of North Uist, was linked by causeway to its larger neighbour in 1998. It is the embarkation point for the ferry connection to Harris. Although only small, about 5km long and 3km wide, there is plenty of variety in terms of scenery and historical interest. The walk described here combines the wonderful beach and machair country on the west side of the island with visits to some of the historical sites in the interior and on the east coast. The route is described in a clockwise direction to benefit from the prevailing south-westerly wind and the magnificent views northwards as you stroll along the beach. It is wise to start the circuit at low tide when there is plenty of firm sand to walk on. When crossing crofting land, keep to the edge of the fenced areas to avoid disturbing livestock.

En route to Berneray, it is worth stopping near Dùn an Sticir (NF 897 777), 2km south-west of the causeway. The dun itself, located on an islet in Loch an Sticir, is relatively well preserved, with a substantial rock causeway.

▸ Exit the car park via a stile over the northern perimeter fence. Follow the fence and marker posts to your left before making a short detour to visit the Chair Stone (NF 909 815), a possible remnant of a Viking court. Now trend in a north-westerly direction across the machair, heading for the ridge of sand dunes. This is excellent walking country, the springy turf providing great cushioning for the feet. As you approach the dune crest, the deep marram is slightly more challenging, but you soon reach the beach, an inviting expanse of white sand. Walk north-east along this wonderful stretch with views west to **Boreray** and **Pabbay**. Later, as the coastline curves

Berneray was the birthplace, in 1825, of Giant MacAskill, who is widely regarded as the world's largest 'true' giant. He stood 2.36m tall and wore boots 44cm long.

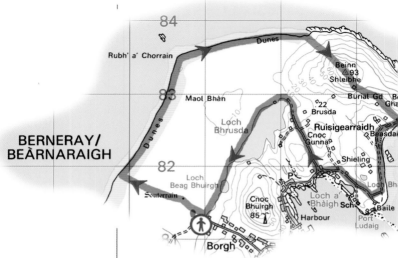

**BERNERAY/
BEÀRNARAIGH**

round, the Harris
hills provide a majestic back-drop. The lower beach
is also an absorbing scene, the incessant power of the
giant, rolling waves contrasting with the frenzied activity
of diminutive waders darting back and forth.

After approximately 3km, a rocky outcrop of white
pegmatite rock marks the end of the beach (NF 923 837).
Now head inland, following marker posts south-east
along an old fence line. A short, steep climb brings you
to the trig point on **Beinn Shleibhe**, the highest point on
Berneray, and more superlative views, now including the
east side of the island. From the summit, marker posts
guide you down through a gate beside a **burial ground**
and then around the edge of the grazing land, through
another gate to the road (NF 934 826).

The next section of the route follows the road, but
you may initially prefer to take to the sand once more.
The road swings sharply right, past some restored
thatched houses and a larger house, the birthplace of
Sir Norman Macleod, an important figure from the 17th
century. Continue along the road by the shore, keeping a

look-out for seals. You will see many ruined black houses, relics of past days when Berneray's population stood well above the present figure of 136.

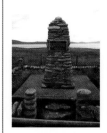

At the junction (NF 925 819), fork right along the road leading into the interior of the island. Go straight on over the rise and then down the track heading north, continuing through a gate near the head of **Loch Bhrusda**. Shortly after passing the loch, the track changes direction, now heading south-west. Follow this route across cultivated croft land, and, as you pass close to the loch side, you will almost certainly be serenaded by a gaggle of greylag geese. The way continues south, past a sheep fank (sheep pen) and a small lochan, named on the map as **Loch Beag Bhuirgh**. Finally, the windmill beside the community hall guides you back to your starting point.

Monument to Giant MacAskill (NF 896 802)

One use for the way markers!

WALK 1.2
Udal

Start/Finish	Picnic site/car park just off the A865 at Greinetobht (NF 819 756)
Distance	8km
Total Ascent	100m
Time	3–4hrs
Terrain	Machair and sandy coast
Maps	OS Explorer 454; OS Landranger 18

The peninsula containing Udal and Àird a' Mhòrain protrudes north towards the island of Boreray, and is the northernmost extension of the Isle of North Uist. This stretch of sand and machair is a tombolo, a sand spit which has been slowly extended by coastal deposition, creating a bridge to a former offshore island. This walk takes in beaches and machair on both sides of the peninsula and also visits an important site of archaeological interest.

Use of the more detailed OS Explorer map for this particular walk is problematic because the route requires the use of both sides of the sheet. The 1:50,000 Landranger map may be more suitable.

Follow the track north from the picnic site to a shallow estuary crossed by a ford. There should be small stepping-stones visible to help you across, but if the tide is high, there is an alternative route. Go inland for a short distance, through a gate, and then, at the first opportunity, return back through another gate to the shore. From here, the route curves generally north-east for almost 2km towards the neck of land, **Corran Àird a' Mhòrain**. The firm surface of the upper beach is excellent for walking, and there are great views north-east across the sands to the Harris hills. ◄

Closer at hand, when the tide is out, you are treated to the spellbinding patterns of tidal ripple marks: nature's fingerprints.

As you approach the end of the beach, a track strikes back inland across the machair. Go north, following this track for about 700m, but as you near the shore again, drop down once more to sea level. At low tide, a vast expanse of sand is unveiled before you. Further on, the sand gives way to shingle and larger fragments of gneiss, rounded by constant attrition. This surface is much more of a challenge to both feet and ankles, and it is advisable to escape inland again.

There is now a choice of route. If you wish to visit the **cemetery**, the burial place for the MacLeans of nearby Boreray, opt for the track heading east-north-east. A marker post on a small headland guides you round to the cemetery (NF 837 787). After the visit, trend north-west across rolling dunes, up to the **trig point**. If you prefer to go directly to the trig point, the way lies initially over an almost flat area of machair, decorated by wild flowers in spring and summer. At the foot of the final rise, about 100m inland from Tràigh Udal, a gate provides access to the slope ahead.

The route passes close to **deep depressions** of bare sand – natural excavations, often initiated by burrowing rabbits, but later enlarged by the relentless blasting of the merciless wind. Closer examination reveals some fascinating artwork: small, stranded pebbles with their wind-sculpted tails, like a miniature scene from one of the world's great deserts.

Tràigh Udal

Ascend the steep dunes to the trig point (NF 831 791), **Àird a' Mhòrain**. Close by, to the north, is **Boreray** and its deserted settlement. Turning south, the view on a clear, sunny day is breathtaking, a spread of white sand directly below, curling round to a rocky headland. Descend and enjoy the spectacle: oystercatchers parading around the shallows and gulls dodging the incoming breakers. At the southern end of the beach, head back inland and follow a path south-west. After about 300m you reach a mound on your left, with a fenced-off enclosure (NF 825 783). This is the site of a wheelhouse dating from the Iron Age: a good, well-preserved example.

After examining the wheelhouse, continue, still in a south-westerly direction, along a clearly defined grassy track to the place marked **Udal**. A ridge of dunes rises to the right, clothed in deep marram grass. Follow the base of this ridge for about 500m, and then, as the track nears the shore, cut across to the dune crest (NF 821 773) where you will be greeted by yet another superb view – a pristine beach curling round towards **Vallay**. This shoreline is a superb place for a variety of recreational activities.

It seems a shame to leave such an appealing environment, but after approximately 1km, you need to strike back inland. The passage through the dunes is probably easier if you can find a blow-out: a natural corridor through the ridge where the sand has been displaced. Once over the dunes, you soon regain the track, continuing south past cultivated fields. Shortly the track veers left, cutting between the fields, back to the eastern shore. From here, a brief walk leads back to the picnic site.

WALK 1.3
Crògearraidh Mòr

Start/Finish	Just north of Loch Aonghais (NF 857 741)
Distance	3km; 4km including Maari (the next hill)
Total Ascent	180m; 250m for both hills
Time	2hrs
Terrain	Hill
Maps	OS Explorer 454; OS Landranger 18

This is a small rocky hill in the northern part of North Uist, easily recognisable from a distance. Its ascent is worthwhile for the fine views over Berneray and Vallay, but it has an added attraction; unlike some of the larger hills further east, which require long approach walks, the round trip up and down Crògearraidh Mòr takes less than 2hrs. The climb is especially good on a summer evening, when the long hours of daylight provide enough time for an after-dinner ramble as the sun begins to set over the western horizon. The hill is climbed most easily from the Solas to Lochmaddy road near Loch Aonghais and, if time permits, may be combined with its neighbour, Maari.

From the roadside near Loch Aonghais, follow the broad track inland towards the two hills. Depending on the season, the next section may prove interesting

on account of livestock, eager to make your acquaintance. If unnerved, you could enquire at the nearby house whether it is safe to proceed. If all is well, go through the gate and pass through the field ahead. Continue through two more gates, allowing clear access to the hillside. The track continues to a point just above the 60m contour, and from there, although any route is possible, it is wise to deviate to the right to avoid the old peat cuttings with their sudden steep drops and pools of stagnant water.

Perhaps the most obvious choice of route extends the line of the track up to the saddle, **Bealach Maari**, between the two hills, then turns north-east and climbs steeply up assorted grass, rock and heather to the top of **Crògearraidh Mòr**. On this final section there are scrambling options available to those who prefer an additional challenge. However, whichever way you advance, a solid rock

Loch Aonghais and dun with Crògearraidh Mòr

Looking south-east from the top of Crògearraidh Mòr towards Eabhal

pavement with veins of milky quartz heralds your arrival at the summit. ▶

The way back down is straightforward, although the steep descent from the top requires care. After returning to the bealach, either descend directly north-west to regain the track, or head south-west past a **standing stone** (NF 864 729) to the slightly lower additional summit of **Maari**. From there, a moderately steep descent north over grass and heather brings you down to the road.

There are good views from here and, if the sky is clear in the west, it should be possible to distinguish not only the St Kilda group as a whole, but the individual islands of Hirta and Boreray.

WALK 1.4
Lochportain

Start/Finish	North of the cattle grid beside Loch an t-Sagairt (NF 949 722)
Distance	9km
Total Ascent	250m
Time	4–5hrs
Terrain	Hill and rocky coast
Maps	OS Explorer 454; OS Landranger 18
Access	Head east down the Lochportain road, from the junction 6km north-west of Lochmaddy.

A fine and varied walk into the extreme north-eastern region of North Uist – an area rarely visited, except by the occasional intrepid angler. The route encounters both moorland and coastal habitats and provides a good opportunity to see eagles and other wildlife. There are also a number of features of historical interest, and the walk may be extended to visit an abandoned settlement at Camas Crùbaig (NF 944 708).

This route has an arguable advantage over some of the other moorland walks in that it includes only intermittent, relatively short sections of ascent. However, good navigational skills are required, and sturdy, waterproof footwear is strongly recommended.

Walk around the northern side of the small quarry adjacent to the cattle grid, and then cross a flat, marshy stretch of ground to reach the northern shore of **Loch na Caiginn**. Near the opposite side of the loch, on an islet, you will see the remains of an Iron Age dun. Now continue around the eastern shore of the loch, then follow a south-south-westerly course up a moderate incline to the northern end of **Loch Thacleit**. There are sheep and deer tracks for short distances, but their quality and reliability are sometimes questionable. The way now goes due south along the eastern side of first Loch Thacleit, and then **Loch Grota** – enjoyable walking on sound terrain, with fine views gradually developing across Loch nam Madadh to Lì a Tuath.

If you wish to visit the abandoned village of **Camas Crùbaig**, first head west just north of Loch Thacleit, and then follow a line of cliffs south-west down to the shore. After exploring the ruins, abandoned in the early 20th century, you may intercept the original route by tracking along the coast to reach the lighthouse at **Rubha an Fhigheadair** (NF 955 691).

If you are not taking the diversion to Camas Crùbaig, after passing the southern end of Loch Grota, it is wise to maintain height before contouring around the slopes above **Loch na Bèiste**. To the west, the extensive area of Loch nam Madadh is the setting for numerous islands, their shapes constantly changing as the tides ebb and flow. Continue due south around the side of **Beinn Sgàpar** and past a small lochan at NF 951 697. Over the rise ahead you can look down to Loch Sgàpal and further south across the bay to Madadh Mòr. Descend to the shingle beach below, then follow the coast round to reach the end of the outward journey, the lighthouse at Rubha an Fhigheadair (NF 955 691). Just offshore you see Madadh Beag, its rocky surface frequented by cormorants and shags.

View west from the slopes of Beinn Sgàpar to Crògearraidh Mòr

The **'Maddies'** (Na Madaidhean) are the rocky islets near the entrance to Loch nam Madadh from which the sea loch and village derived their names. The name translates as 'Loch of the Hounds'.

The hinterland behind the cliffs is good eagle country, and there is a fair chance of sighting these majestic birds.

The initial part of the return journey follows the coastline north-east. Care is required, as there are steep, rocky cliffs, often penetrating well inland. Looking back south, you now see all three 'Maddies' with their striking profiles, forged when basaltic lava was forced up into the gneiss. ◄

After about 2km, as you approach **Loch Scalan**, you will notice an obvious cave entrance on the hillside further west (NF 961 709). Ascend the steep hillside to reach the cave and, after a brief inspection, break out to the hillside above, heading north-west. After passing the southern end of **Loch Gille ghoid**, head west to reach the saddle south of **Beinn Thacleit**. Beneath you, further west, lies Loch Thacleit, passed earlier on the journey. From the saddle, make a descending traverse northwards across the western slopes of Beinn Thacleit. You pass old ruins, probable evidence of early settlement, and also gain a fine aerial perspective of the dun and its adjoining causeway. Presently, you return to the shores of Loch na Caiginn, and from there a short walk leads back to the road.

The cave at NF 961 709

WALK 1.5
Lì a Tuath and Lì a Deas

Start/Finish	A small parking place beside the Lochmaddy-Clachan main road, 3km out of Lochmaddy (opposite the transmission mast) (NF 900 682)
Distance	Lì a Tuath 11km; both hills 14km
Total Ascent	300m; 500m
Time	4hrs; 5–7hrs
Terrain	Hill and moor
Maps	OS Explorer 454; OS Landranger 18

The walk to Lì a Tuath and Lì a Deas, the hills which overlook Lochmaddy, is challenging on several counts: the ground is virtually pathless, and the going is genuinely tough, a mixture of blanket bog, rocky slabs and deep heather – excellent yomping country. Navigation is difficult even on a clear day, and a map and compass, or GPS, are essential equipment. However, there are memorable rewards: two different eagles, golden and white-tailed, may readily be encountered along the route, and red deer are often observed at close quarters. It is definitely worth packing your binoculars.

▶ Cross the road from the parking place and follow the verge south-west to where a stile provides access to the moor. Continue around a small loch, past some shooting butts, and then head due south, gradually descending across pasture to a gate and sheepfold at the head of the bay (NF 902 678).

Go through the gate and round the shore before ascending the rise ahead in a south-easterly direction (Explorer map spot height 29m). This is a useful point from which to observe the route ahead, and also note that the general direction is south-east towards the distant summit of Lì a Tuath. From the rise, the least complicated route cuts east for 200m around the end of the loch ahead, and then veers south-east for 900m across marshy peatland: an almost featureless, forlorn landscape with only the occasional hummock to provide relief. The

In summer 2014, marker posts were installed to provide an alternative route to the top of Lì a Tuath. The posts begin about 200m further south of the start described in the text.

target is the isthmus at NF 911 671, where stepping-stones ford a small burn, but you will have to thread a way around various lochans before you reach your destination.

Almost immediately beyond the stones, cross a wooden fence

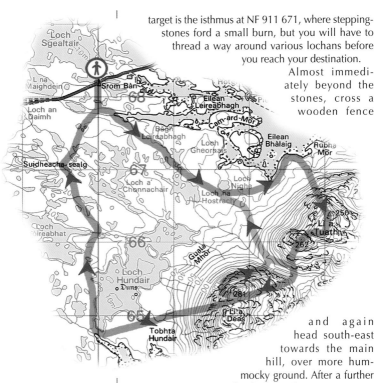

and again head south-east towards the main hill, over more hummocky ground. After a further 500m, a gap leads through a cross-cutting fence. Continue through this gap, past assorted debris, and now strike uphill to where a gate allows access to the north side of the adjacent fence. Much drier walking across heather and grass, now in a generally north-westerly direction, brings you round to the coastline at NF 925 672, across the bay from the Lochmaddy ferry terminal. This is the starting point for the annual Beinn Lee Hill Race and our walk follows the route of this race to the top of Lì a Tuath. From the shore, head south-south-east up gently sloping ground beside the fence. The route gradually leaves the fence line, moving over steeper terrain towards a broad, open gully flanking the north side of the hill.

Climb this gully to where the gradient eases, and now scramble up to the right over a short section of steep heather and rock. The gradient soon eases again, and presently, after a short ascent, you arrive at the **trig point** (NF 931 663). This is a timely place for a rest, and a good vantage point for watching the Calmac ferry as it embarks on the journey to Uig in Skye. A broad ridge leads south-west from the trig point towards the main summit of **Lì a Tuath**. As you traverse this ridge, a steep, rocky face ahead blocks progress. The easiest line is to trend left around the end of this face, and then cut sharply back right, up a rocky shoulder, to reach the highest point.

Descend the southern slopes of the hill towards the **dam** at the eastern end of the small reservoir (NF 925 656) that occupies the narrow trench of Bealach a' Sgail. This section is relatively steep, but also very rocky, and huge slabby outcrops of gneiss cover much of the hillside.

Lì a Tuath

When only moderately steep, the rock can offer a sound, stable downhill passage. However, when wet, the lichen-covered surfaces may become slippery and dangerous. In these conditions it is wiser to opt for an alternative route over the grass and heather.

To return home from this point, walk west along the north side of the reservoir and then, from the dam, continue over the brow of the hill towards the north-west. A fence, broken by a gate, gives access to the pasture below. Descend for 800m, generally following the fence line on your right, to a break in the fence in front (NF 916 667). You can now retrace your steps from the outward journey: first north-west for 500m to the stepping-stones, and then onwards, continuing north-west across the marshy ground back to the head of the inlet at NF 902 678. Go through the gate by the sheepfold and then head north-west past small lochans to the main road.

This is great deer and eagle country, with a glorious sense of isolation.

For those who wish to continue on from Lì a Tuath to **Lì a Deas**, the least demanding route of ascent from the dam is via the eastern slopes of the hill, where gently sloping, heathery gullies lead up to higher ground. Nevertheless, despite the shallow gradient, the heather is seriously deep for anyone who is short in stature. ◀

Upward progress continues over a broad, rocky shoulder and small rock steps offer excellent scrambling, if desired. The summit is reached surprisingly quickly, the small cairn perhaps an indication of how few people visit this place.

The easiest descent route continues south-west from the cairn for approximately 100m, then cuts down to the right to reach the top of a long grassy ramp. Follow this ramp to its foot, descending in a north-easterly direction across the side of the hill. Now contour across beside a fence until a gate provides access to the pasture below. From this point, follow the directions given for the return journey from the reservoir.

A longer and more arduous alternative for enthusiastic bogtrotters goes around the southern end of **Loch Hundair**, but adds approximately 2km to the distance.

After leaving the summit of Lì a Deas, head south-west for about 250m until you intercept a burn flowing westwards to the loch. Follow the burn for 300m and then continue in a westerly direction to cross the isthmus separating Loch Hundair from the sea (NF 901 647).

The next 3.5km, in a very unlikely straight line back to the mast at NF 901 682, is challenging – partly on account of the monotonous terrain, but more importantly because navigation is difficult.

> There is one obvious marker that you may encounter, a strange **cairn or standing stone** beside an unnamed lochan, but there are few other noticeable landmarks. The bearing is almost precisely grid north, but there are innumerable barriers along the way, most of them very wet. It is like playing a computer game, where forward progress is constantly being interrupted by yet another fiendish obstacle.

It is almost impossible to give precise instructions, but there are one or two pointers to help navigation: on a clear day you can focus on distant Beinn Mhòr (NF 898 762), and, as you near journey's end, the mast itself becomes visible – a definite boost for weary limbs. If in doubt, it is best to head more to the north-west. In that direction, you will sooner or later reach the main road.

Cairn/standing stone on Lochmaddy moor

WALK 1.6
Langais

Start/Finish	A clearly signed car park at Barpa Langais beside the Lochmaddy–Clachan road, 9km south-west of Lochmaddy (NF 835 658)
Distance	Main walk 3.5km; detours may increase the distance to 6km
Total Ascent	150m
Time	2–3hrs
Terrain	Hill and moor
Maps	OS Explorer 454; OS Landranger 18

This is a relatively short circuit over a small hill, but it includes places of archaeological interest and provides an opportunity for a possible sighting of otters and other wildlife. The walk may be combined with Langass Woods to add an extra botanical dimension, or perhaps to find shelter on a wet and windy day!

Beside the car park, there are displays from the Hebridean Archaeological Interpretation Programme, providing extensive historical information relating to Barpa Langais and the surrounding landscape.

From the car park, a gravel track leads up to the **chambered cairn** of Barpa Langais, believed to be an ancient burial chamber about 5000 years old. The entrance to the barp, on the south-east side, is still remarkably well preserved. However, although inviting, entry is not recommended – the evidence of subsidence on the top of the cairn spells out a clear warning! Barpa Langais is the best-preserved Neolithic chambered cairn in the Western Isles. It was probably used for communal burials, and early excavations over a century ago revealed cremated human bones.

After inspecting the barp, proceed gently upwards across the moor. A line of marker posts leads to the trig point at the top of the hill – relatively

straightforward walking, but the trick is to avoid the wet bits. Also, on Saturdays in the autumn and winter, beware of the stampeding members of North Uist Amateur Athletics Club honing their cross-country skills. Feel free to join in!

As you continue south-east from the top of **Beinn Langais**, the view is impressive; the long, linear settlement of Loch Euphort and its emerald-green swathe of reseeding is seen stretching out towards Eabhal and Burabhal in the distance. The area around Loch Euphort was almost uninhabited until the late 19th century, when it was settled by crofters who had been cleared off their land near Solas, 20km to the north-west.

Near the top of the hill a path veers off to the left, to the edge of a forestry plantation, Langass Woods, a worthwhile diversion. ▶ The forest, which was originally planted back in the 1950s, is now the focus of a community initiative. Gravel tracks are being constructed through the trees, and there are information notices to help identify sites of particular archaeological and biological interest.

In Langass Woods, at NF 846 654, there is a carved wooden statue of Hercules, the grizzly bear who went missing whilst on a trip to Uist in 1980.

'Leac Alasdair' in Langass Woods

The forest may also be accessed separately from a car park beside the main road at NF 854 658.

From an unusual gate cutting through the perimeter fence at NF 845 654, various paths head down through the trees. A short exploration will give you a taste of this habitat, a contrast to the open moors. Cones and pine needles litter the forest floor, and there are also abundant fungi. In a large clearing, the result of storm damage, secondary colonisation has provided new plant species. After a tour of the forest, retrace your steps uphill to the stile and out onto the open moorland. The markers take you back to the main path, and then the route descends the hill, trending right to reach a **stone circle**, Sornach Coir' Fhìnn (NF 843 649). ◄

The stone circle dates from the second millennium BC, and consists of a total of approximately 40 stones, although only 24 remain upright.

Another diversion, to look for otters, follows a faint path south-east from the circle to the coastline opposite the small islands at NF 846 646. One of the best times to observe these elusive animals is when the tide is rising. Otter spotting walks led by local experts are arranged weekly between May and August (contact Jamie Boyle on 07768 042547).

Returning to the stone circle, the path continues through two tall gates and then along the road, past the **Langass Lodge Hotel**. About 200m beyond the hotel, almost opposite a junction, a vague track climbs up the hillside to the right. Marker posts lead you back to the barp and then down to the car park.

WALK 1.7

Burabhal

Start/Finish	Car park at Loch Euphort road end (NF 891 631)
Distance	Burabhal 6km; the cave 8km; extended walk 12km
Total Ascent	150m; 200m; 250m
Time	3hrs; 4–5hrs; 6–7hrs
Terrain	Hill and rocky coast
Maps	OS Explorer 454; OS Landranger 18, 22

As you face east from the car park at Loch Euphort road end, Burabhal is the central hill with the flat-topped summit. Although dwarfed by its loftier neighbours to the north and south, Burabhal is a very worthwhile alternative, and its ascent may be comfortably achieved in a morning or afternoon outing. The view from the top provides ample reward for the exertion, particularly looking west, where sea lochs invade far inland, almost bisecting the island of North Uist. The route described here ascends Burabhal itself, and two longer options are outlined which extend the walk right across to the east coast. The extended route includes two unusual landscape features – a cave at NF 915 615 and the natural arch at NF 927 607 – and also allows the walker to experience the contrasting wildlife habitats of moor and coast.

Explorer 454 is the recommended map, as this walk crosses the boundary between two Landranger maps.

Leaving the car park, follow the track east through a gate and across pasture. The track continues over a small rise and then descends past a bay with a miniature stone pier. At the eastern end of the bay bear right across marshy ground, then follow a rough path leading to **stepping-stones** at NF 898 631.

The short, steep ascent up Burabhal

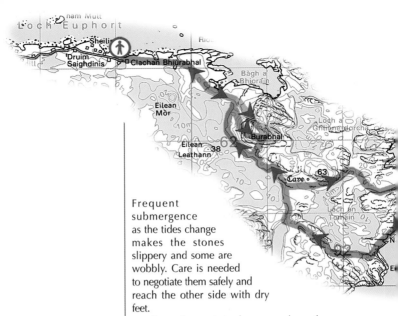

Frequent submergence as the tides change makes the stones slippery and some are wobbly. Care is needed to negotiate them safely and reach the other side with dry feet.

From the eastern shore, go along the path past a ruined shieling and continue across uneven, boggy terrain. The track is hard to follow precisely, but some large boulders in the distance provide a useful direction marker. The walking is generally good, but progress is occasionally blocked by wet, peaty gullies; these are not a major obstacle, but skill at long jump could prove useful. The route becomes clearer again as you approach the fence beneath **Burabhal**, and this fence is easily crossed close to **Loch Obasaraigh** (NF 905 626). Two main routes of ascent go up from the fence. The more gradual option is to follow the track around the shore for 400m, and then scale the grass and heathery shoulder above **Loch Obasaraigh**. The convex upper slopes contrive to keep the summit hidden until the very end, but eventually you arrive on a grassy plateau topped by a small cairn.

A steeper and more direct approach tackles the shallow gully leading to the rocky escarpment on the north side of the summit. The cliffs that form this escarpment may be avoided at either end by climbing steep grass to the top.

For those who wish to return home after Burabhal, it is best to return west down the more gradual way of ascent. The path by the shore takes you back over the fence and continues to the stepping-stones, and thence to the car park.

For those who wish to extend the walk to the cave, descending in a different direction will save time, although care must be taken on the steep, rocky hillside. At the summit turn south-west to face the dark silhouette of Eabhal glowering over Loch Obasaraigh. After walking a few metres in this direction, a short diversion to the left leads around a small crag to where the ground flattens out. Continue 100m towards the south-west and descend a narrow, steep and grassy rake between the rock outcrops until the ground levels again. Turning first right and then sharp left, you can now follow a ramp downwards, following the base of the cliffs in a south-south-easterly direction. After descending for about 200m, a shallow valley leads right to meet the path above Loch Obasaraigh (NF 910 617).

Proceed south-east, following this path for about 500m until you reach a very small, sandy bay. From this bay, strike abruptly left along the base of a rise to reach a flat, marshy area. Ahead is a line of cliffs and, near the left-hand end, a green apron of grass marks the base of the **cave** entrance (NF 915 614). The cave certainly warrants a closer inspection, and a short, boggy walk brings you to the foot of rocks immediately below the entrance. To investigate further, care is required, especially in damp conditions, and it is important to remember that, although the ascent may seem straightforward, the descent is often more treacherous. After clambering up rocks and then steep grass you discover an impressive opening, only 5m across, but penetrating almost 30m into the mountainside – a fine venue for a highland gathering!

eig Mhòr

*The cave at
NF 915 614*

Returning to ground level, there are two options. To get back to the start, you will need to retrace your recent steps back to the path along the shore of Loch Obasaraigh, and then head back north-west, following the path round the shore to the fence before eventually reaching the stepping-stones and then onwards to the car park.

For the continuation to the arch you must trend south-east from the cave along the foot of the cliffs, down to the shore of **Loch an Tomain** (NF 917 614). Sheep tracks now provide great walking along the loch side in a north-easterly direction. On reaching the head of the loch, leave the water's edge, and first travel south-east and then east to follow a burn down to the coast. The walk along the cliff south from here is delightful: dramatic rock scenery and an assortment of headlands and rocky inlets to sustain interest. Near the clifftop fulmars dance close attendance on unwelcome visitors, while cormorants and shags preside over the rocky promenade closer to the crashing waves. It is wise to move with caution; some of the rock is loose and slippery, and help is a long distance away.

The **natural arch** cannot be seen from afar and appears almost unexpectedly. It is easier to locate by first finding the small lochan at NF 926 607 before moving back to the coast. The arch is relatively small, but easy to access, and it provides a photogenic frame for an image of distant Skye.

For the return journey, it is best to head inland to the shore of Loch an Tomain and continue its circumnavigation in a clockwise direction. Sheep and deer tracks aid progress through the deep heather and bracken, and the many islets in the loch ensure an absorbing view, a constantly changing interplay of land and water. ▶

Deer are always close by, and in autumn the landscape becomes a fleeting home for thousands of caterpillars.

Moving around the southern end of the loch, veer north-west towards the distant gap between Eabhal and Burabhal. There are many undulations along the way, but the expanse of **Loch Surtavat** soon appears at the foot of Eabhal. Follow the burn draining from the northern end of this loch and continue along its course to the beach beside Loch Obasaraigh. From there, the path takes you back to the start.

EABHAL

Eabhal, the highest hill in North Uist, rises prominently above the surrounding landscape, and its distinctive profile dominates the horizon as you travel north from Benbecula. Although, at 347m, Eabhal is relatively modest in height, the long approaches over uneven terrain make the ascent a deceptively strenuous outing. Nevertheless, despite the effort, the climb up Eabhal is one of the best walks in the Uists, and on a clear day there are extensive views over an extraordinary landscape where land and water intermingle in a collage of blues, browns, greys and greens. Red deer are common in this part of North Uist, and in the autumn rutting season the bellowing sound of stags may be heard reverberating across the hillsides. The hill itself is almost completely surrounded by water, with sea to the south and east, and Loch Obasaraigh blocking approaches from the north and west. Careful study of the map is required to reveal narrow necks of land breaching these watery defences.

There are two main routes up Eabhal: one from Saighdinis at the end of the Loch Euphort road, the other from Cladach Chairinis. Both of these routes are described and each is rewarding in its own right. However, an interesting and more varied option, if suitable transport is available, is to combine the two, starting at Saighdinis (NF 891 631) and traversing Eabhal to finish at Cladach Chairinis (NF 856 589).

When planning the walk there are two points to note. Firstly, navigation using the OS Landranger 1:50,000 maps may be problematical because the Loch Euphort route sits astride the boundary between sheets 18 and 22. It is much easier to use the OS 1:25,000 Explorer Map for North Uist and Berneray. Secondly, it is important to check the tides before setting out. Near the beginning of the walk, it is necessary to cross stepping-stones, which may be submerged at high tide. As the tides ebb and flow, the surge of water flowing through the narrow gap is significant, and a misjudgement of time and tide on the return from Eabhal may necessitate an unwelcome delay on the eastern bank. Consult the tourist information office in Lochmaddy (tel. 01876 500321) for tidal information.

WALK 1.8
Eabhal from Loch Euphort

Start/Finish	Car park at Loch Euphort road end (NF 891 631)
Distance	11km; 12km for the traverse of Eabhal
Total Ascent	350m
Time	4–5hrs
Terrain	Hill and moor
Maps	OS Explorer 454; OS Landranger 18, 22
Access	Leave the main Clachan–Lochmaddy double track at a junction 1km north-east of Clachan.

As you drive east along the Loch Euphort road, the principal hills of North Uist are aligned before you along a north-south axis: Lì a Tuath, Lì a Deas, Burabhal and finally Eabhal.

The approach march to the foot of Eabhal follows the northern shore of Loch Obasaraigh, skirting around the base of Burabhal. Eabhal itself is tackled by ascending the broad east ridge. The walk is interesting on account of its continuously changing landscape and geology.

▶ From the car park, follow the directions given in Walk 1.7 as far as the fence crossing at NF 905 626. From here, a distinct, if somewhat muddy, path follows the northern shore of the loch and after 2km reaches a sandy beach (NF 912 611). The mouth of a small burn sometimes blocks immediate access to the beach. If this is a problem, it is much easier to cross slightly further upstream. The beach, which lies almost at the foot of Eabhal, is an ideal place for a picnic, and provides a good vantage point for studying the route ahead.

Close to the car park, along a short path to the south-west, there is a sculpture of deer antlers, part of the local Art on the Map initiative.

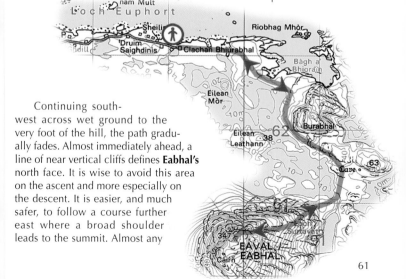

Continuing south-west across wet ground to the very foot of the hill, the path gradually fades. Almost immediately ahead, a line of near vertical cliffs defines **Eabhal's** north face. It is wise to avoid this area on the ascent and more especially on the descent. It is easier, and much safer, to follow a course further east where a broad shoulder leads to the summit. Almost any

61

The beach at the eastern end of Loch Obasaraigh

route is possible, but near the bottom, where the ground is steeper, it is often necessary to zigzag between the rocky outcrops. In the middle section, as the gradient decreases, the more gently sloping rocky slabs often provide a drier and more agreeable alternative to the wetter surroundings. As you approach the top, the ground steepens again and a broad, grassy gully is the obvious route of ascent. Gradually, the gradient eases and soon the summit, with its trig point and surrounding stone shelter, is attained.

When the air is clear, the view from the summit of **Eabhal** is extensive. Beyond the intricate pattern of land and water surrounding Eabhal, there are more distant views of islands in every direction. Following the compass round from Harris in the north, next comes Skye to the east and then Benbecula and South Uist. Finally, out in the Atlantic, on the western horizon, lies St Kilda.

If you wish to carry on to make a traverse of Eabhal, follow the descent directions given in Walk 1.9. Otherwise, it is time to head homeward.

The descent retraces the outward route, but it is important to avoid the cliffs on the northern slopes and head first in an easterly direction. Descend slowly, as there are many small cliffs hidden from above, and be wary of sheep tracks, which may appear promising but often prove hazardous. The sheep's intelligence may be questionable, but its abilities on steep terrain would put most of us to shame.

After reaching the northern end of **Loch Surtavat** (NF 912 608), follow the burn flowing to Loch Obasaraigh. Now retrace your steps around the shores of the loch and, after the fence, follow the track past the large boulders and back to the stepping-stones. Two different tracks leave from the opposite side. Both will take you back to the start, but the northern route, although less direct, is probably drier.

WALK 1.9
Eabhal from Cladach Chairinis

Start/Finish	Beside the turning space at Cladach Chairinis road end (NF 856 589). Take care not to block the turning area when parking.
Distance	12km
Total Ascent	350m
Time	4–5hrs
Terrain	Hill and moor
Maps	OS Explorer 454; OS Landranger 22
Access	The road to Cladach Chairinis branches off the North Uist–Benbecula main road, 2km south of Cairinis.

This route up Eabhal perhaps has less scenic variety than the Loch Euphort walk, but there is ample compensation in the form of wildlife and historical sites. However, navigation is very challenging in misty conditions, and it is wise to choose a clear day when Eabhal itself guides you across the moor and the summit views will be better. The walk crosses broad areas of spongy peat bog – a stern test for waterproof footwear.

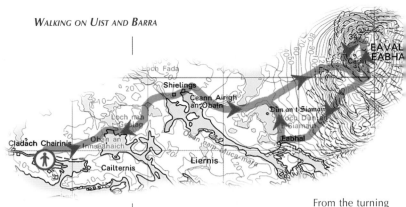

From the turning area where the tarmac road ends, continue past a white house (the former primary school) and branch off to the left, following the track down towards the thatched cottage. Continue past the left side of the cottage and then onwards, towards distant Eabhal, bypassing some old peat cuttings. For the first 2km, until you reach the **shielings** at NF 873 598, it is helpful to use the summit of Eabhal as a direction indicator. Bearing this in mind, proceed north-east around the right flank of the small rounded hill immediately ahead. A path is discernible in places and for a short passage follows a natural

Eabhal from Cladach Chairinis

rocky causeway. After passing the hill, the route gradually descends towards the shore and then picks up another path leading to an old rusty gate (NF 865 593) about 1km from the start.

As you pass the sheltered coves and inlets, do not be tempted to venture out across the inter-tidal areas of sand close to shore, as there are patches of sinking sand.

Cross a burn by some strategically placed stepping-stones and then, still focusing on Eabhal, go through a gate in the fence immediately ahead. Now, mount the rising ground until a small cairn is visible, 400m distant. Marshy ground takes you to this cairn, and another cairn, topped by a fence post, comes into view. From the second cairn you should be able to identify the ruined houses and shielings clearly marked on the OS map. Go past the ruins along a path above the shoreline, now veering round towards the south-east. ▶

The path gradually fades, but a gate, which should be clearly visible ahead, is the next target. Beyond the gate, the path reappears for a short time, leading through deep heather to a narrow loch (NF 879 597) and then rising gradually above the right shore. Continue round the loch towards Eabhal itself and then on to another gate near the southern end of **Loch Obasaraigh** (NF 883 596). The approach is over; now for the climb.

Trending to the left around a hillock with large angular boulders, you are now at the foot of Eabhal and ahead lies open hillside. It is worth scanning the ground and sky carefully, ideally with binoculars. Deer frequent this area and golden eagles may also be seen soaring majestically over their chosen domain. A good line from here follows the burn about 100m right of the obvious ruin (cairns marked on OS Explorer map). There is no definite path and you can alternate between banks to find the easiest walking. Bear round to the right, tracking the burn up as far as the col between the hills ahead. Near the source of the burn, the ground flattens in an area dissected by peaty gullies. From here, make a rising traverse left for about 200m to the foot of a long, rocky escarpment and a small cliff of pink feldspar. Continue right, following the

Along this stretch you may see empty mussel shells littering the ground, the discarded leftovers from scavenging gulls.

base of the escarpment to the top of the rise where, on a clear, sunny day, a wonderful view unfolds: east to Skye with Waterstein Head, Macleod's Tables and the Cuillin, and south-east to the conical peaks of Rum.

A cairn, on rocks up to the left, marks the continuation of the route. Facing towards the top of Eabhal from this point you will notice an obvious subsidiary summit. Follow a line 100m to the right of this summit, and also detour round the rocky knoll further ahead. Continue a further 200m in the same direction and you will reach the summit trig point and accompanying shelter, a welcome refuge in a south-westerly gale!

The following section describes the way down and also details the second half of the traverse of Eabhal, from Loch Euphort to Cladach Chairinis Walk (1.8).

To descend, head south-south-west to the subsidiary cairned summit (NF 898 603), and then continue south for a further 300m to another cairn standing prominently on a rocky platform. From here, a small lochan (NF 896 598) comes into view – the next destination. Descend south-east from the cairn, and then south-west down rock and steep grass, until the ground levels off. Cross the col and go through a gap between two small hills. There in

Red deer frequent the Eabhal area

the hollow immediately ahead is the lochan: dark, deep and forbidding, but nevertheless a tranquil and sheltered spot. The climb over the rise above the south-east side of the lochan reveals the view down to the abandoned **Eabhal** settlement (NF 888 591), nestling on a narrow isthmus between fresh and salt water. In certain lights one can also make out the linear pattern of lazy beds where cultivation once took place. The drop down to the buildings is quite steep, but the grass and heather underfoot are soft and forgiving, and progress to the bottom is surprisingly quick.

> The **Eabhal** settlement was in the past the home of the local shepherd and his family. It is seemingly remote and isolated, and yet the children crossed the moor, barefoot, twice daily to attend the school in Cladach Chairinis. One local story tells of a former shepherd, out on the hill, who was attacked by a wild cat. As the ferocious beast went for his throat, he was saved by a scarf tied around his neck.
>
> Today local crofters use the cluster of buildings only occasionally, for shearing and dipping their sheep.

From the buildings, head north along the eastern shore of Loch Dùn an t-Siamain for 300m. A stone causeway leads out to the dun itself, about 50m offshore. After passing the site, continue first north and then west, to the gate at NF 883 596. Here you rejoin your outward route, but route finding is more difficult on the return journey without Eabhal to guide you. Now follow faint tracks to another gate near the western end of a narrow loch (NF 879 597). Go through this gate and head north-west to the ruined shielings. From the second ruin (NF 873 598), track south-west past the shore to reach a small cairn with a fence post. Maintain the same direction to a second cairn and then across flat, marshy ground in line with a low, rounded hill 800m ahead. A fence line with a rusty gate (NF 865 593) should come into view. Pass through this gate and then follow a path around the shore for 200m. Now strike inland, past old peat cuttings, and walk round the south-east side of a gently sloping hillock. A large white house comes into view. Weave around patches of marsh to the parking space beside the house – journey's end.

WALK 1.10

Grimsay (Griomasaigh)

Start/Finish	Beside the road, near the western end of Loch Hornaraigh (NF 863 573)
Distance	2.5km
Total Ascent	Negligible
Time	1–2hrs
Terrain	Moor
Maps	OS Explorer 453; OS Landranger 22

Grimsay is a small island between Benbecula and North Uist. The name is of Norse origin, and means 'Grim's island'. Grimsay was a separate island until 1960, when causeways were constructed to provide transport links to its two larger neighbours. The principal form of employment on the island has traditionally been fishing, particularly for shellfish, and the harbour at Kallin provides a sheltered anchorage for a number of boats. Fresh prawns, crab and lobster may be purchased from various outlets near the harbour.

Grimsay has a number of important historical and archaeological sites. The walk described here visits a wheelhouse dating from the Iron Age. This is an especially good example and was only excavated recently, in the 1990s. This short walk, which may be completed comfortably within a couple of hours, provides a circuit of Loch Hornaraigh, passing the wheelhouse on the way.

A circular road, off the main Benbecula – North Uist spinal route, provides good access to all parts of Grimsay.

Leave the road near the bend (NF 863 573), where a track leads off to a house by the shore. Climb the rise immediately to the north, and then cross a dip, heading in the

direction of Eabhal, the principal hill in North Uist. There are good views south-east along the length of **Loch Hornaraigh**. Pass through the gate on your right and then walk east for a short distance, over a small rise. The wheelhouse is just below the rise on the eastern side. ▶

After exploring the site, you will need to strike north-east for about 100m to find a gate allowing access through the adjacent barbed wire fence. Once past the fence, you may continue along the shore for a while, or head back immediately to the loch side. The loch has a number of islets, some accessed by stone causeways, and an Iron Age fortification, **Dùn Bàn** (NF 870 569). Just beyond Dùn Bàn, you reach the end of the loch and cross an old fence line before turning north-west, back towards the start.

You may return to the start either by the road or beside the loch. However, if you follow the loch side, do

Wheelhouses, sometimes known as aisled roundhouses, have an outer circular wall, inside which are radiating stone piers resembling the spokes of a wheel.

Internal structure of the Iron Age wheelhouse on Grimsay

69

take care! There are small cliffs, and the water is deceptively deep.

The walk may be extended to visit a small lochan on the other side of the road (NF 864 569). This lochan, with its extensive reed beds and waterlilies, may, in season, provide the visitor with interesting photo opportunities.

WALK 1.11
Scolpaig

Start/Finish	At the start of the track to Scolpaig (NF 733 748)
Distance	6km
Total Ascent	150m
Time	3hrs
Terrain	Hill and rocky coast
Maps	OS Explorer 454; OS Landranger 18
Access	From the North Uist circular road, the A865, the track leads off to Scolpaig. A small area for parking is normally available just to the south, beside a sheep fank.

The coastline around Scolpaig and Rubha Ghriminis in the far north-western corner of North Uist is exposed to the Atlantic swell, and this has resulted in the formation of a number of dramatic features of marine erosion: cliffs, arches and steep-sided inlets, or geos as they are known locally. The walk described here goes over Beinn Scolpaig before dropping down to the shore. Although it only follows the coastline for a short distance, less than 2km, it visits a number of impressive sites. The cliffs are not particularly high, reaching about 30m at most, but they merit care and respect; the upper slopes are convex and a slip could prove very dangerous. Suitable footwear offering a good grip is essential.

If approaching the start along the main road from the east, you may observe a couple of points of interest along the way. At NF 747 750 there is a large boulder beside the road, with a small plaque beside it. This hefty lump of gneiss was lifted by the legendary Giant MacAskill. The settlement on the island in Loch Olabhat (NF 747 753) is believed to date from the Neolithic period.

From the starting point, head north-west along the track past **Loch Scolpaig**.

At NF 731 750, in the middle of the loch, there is a small tower, **Macleod's Folly**, built in the early 19th century by Dr Alexander Macleod, the factor for North Uist estate. The folly is built over the site of an Iron Age dun.

Continue along the track between the abandoned farm buildings and then veer right, around the eastern end of **Bàgh Scolpaig**. Ahead lies a gap in the wall, but

Macleod's Folly in Loch Scolpaig

to the right, in the corner of the field, is a gate providing access to the hillside. Pass through this gate and then make a rising traverse rightwards up the heathery slope. After a brief steep section, the ground levels off, providing a sight of the trig point on **Beinn Scolpaig**. Cross the flattish, boggy section ahead past a small lochan, and then up a short rise to the top.

After scanning the western horizon for a glimpse of St Kilda, descend northwards to the coast, near to the peninsula of **Sgeir Oireabhal**. You arrive beside a shingle beach, its pebbles washed, shaped and sorted by the crashing waves. Looking west, an obvious cairn is visible in the distance. As you head towards this cairn, the shoreline assumes a different character: a rocky platform of gently dipping strata, ideal for boulder hopping. Dark rock pools add a further spice to this intriguing obstacle course.

As you approach the cairn, a narrow inlet forces you back inland. The power of the swell often funnels through this narrow rocky fissure, hurling flurries of spume and spindrift well inland. In stormy weather, the foam resembles the surface of a giant witch's cauldron with its swirling mix of saltwater and crushed seaweed. The cairn (NF 732 768), despite being out on the headland, is worth a brief visit. It marks the site of an old fort, **Caisteal Odair**, built on a steep-sided promontory, which must have made it almost impregnable.

Continue generally towards the south-west, but take care when leaving the cairn in this direction – the rocks almost immediately overhang another narrow inlet. After rounding this barrier, it is wise to follow the clifftop, but walk well back from the edge; the grass is often damp and slippery and the convex slopes hide steepening cliffs below. The route passes another beach of large rounded cobbles and, after a further 400m, yet another inlet forces you to divert back inland. Straight ahead at NF 727 765 is a large crater, **Sloc Rubha**, the result of the massive collapse of part of the arch undercutting **Rubha Ghriminis**. Arches from the north-east and south-west meet in this plunging defile, but you would need a rope to descend

into its depths. Good views can be had from above, however.

The northern arch may be viewed from a point on the south-west rim of the crater, beside the end of an old stone wall. To view the southern arch, follow this wall further south-west for a few metres, and then, after reaching some iron stanchions, bear right, keeping back from the clifftop. It is safest, especially in a strong wind, to crawl slowly forward to the cliff edge and peer over to spy the arch entrance down below.

In spite of the exposure and incessant blasting by wind and salt, plants such as thrift appear to thrive in this hostile environment, and although this may appear to be an inhospitable place, you are almost always sure of company! Sea birds such as fulmars and kittiwakes are plentiful, and eager to remind you of their presence. ▶

After admiring the spectacle of the arches, and the seaward view out to Hasgeir, your homeward course proceeds inland, up a gradual incline in a south-easterly direction. Once over the crest of the hill, the way should be clear, across grassland to a gate and then on, through the gap in the wall, back to **Scolpaig farm**.

Tyrolean Traverse across an inlet close to Sloc Rubha

This spectacular coastal environment is a paradise for adventure activities such as abseiling, and also the vertigo-inducing Tyrolean Traverse.

WALK 1.12
Hogha Gearraidh and Hosta

Start/Finish	Near the intersection of minor roads beside a postbox (NF 713 721)
Distance	5km
Total Ascent	150m
Time	2–3hrs
Terrain	Rocky coast and sandy coast
Maps	OS Explorer 454; OS Landranger 18
Access	From the North Uist circular road at the junction near Tigh a' Ghearraidh (NF 718 722).

This relatively short walk visits an impressive coastal feature eroded from the cliffs of North Uist. The blow-hole, or kettle spout as it is known locally, consists of a narrow arch bridging a deep chasm over the Atlantic waves. In very stormy weather, fountains of water gush forth from this orifice. The approach to the blow-hole should be treated with caution; the rocks are sloping and slippery, and a fall from these cliffs could prove fatal.

In the months of May and June, beware also of an electric fence erected to contain livestock in the area.

From the postbox, follow the track towards the shore. On a clear day you should see St Kilda on the horizon, directly ahead. As you approach the coast, the track splits, with the main branch veering left past a prominent shingle beach to a house. Take the right fork, running parallel with the shore, to a gate. Passing through the gate, continue close to the shore for the first 400m, but then veer right, inland,

74

Looking down through the blow-hole

across an old fence line to the top of a small hill, encircled on the map by the 20m contour line (NF 705 727). From this point, the blow-hole is very close, less than 50m away to the north. However, take care as the cliffs are potentially very dangerous. ▶

After visiting the blow-hole, you may return to the start by the same route, or continue the walk towards Hosta.

For Hosta, go west along the clifftop, passing steep-sided inlets, and then descend to reach a small cove at NF 709 727. From here, head inland along the fence line until a gate and then a stile allow access to the adacent field. Returning to the shore, you pass a shingle beach with washed up driftwood and, further inland, battered creels, helpless victims of the Atlantic onslaught. Either continue, following close to the shore, or take a short cut, heading east-north-east, across the neck of the headland. Over the rise ahead, a splendid view awaits you: the fine, curving bay of **Tràigh stir** backed by a line of imposing

A story has been passed down concerning the impending collapse of the arch. It is said that, when a newly married Macdonald couple venture to cross this rock bridge, disaster will strike.

The cliffs near Hosta

dunes. Continue north-east, avoiding the cultivated machair, and, after passing through the gate, drop down to the beach. This is an excellent place to relax, with a picnic site nearby (NF 718 729). The sea looks inviting, but be careful. The water has strong currents and is dangerous for swimming.

To complete the walk, climb over the dune ridge and then amble across the flowery machair to the road near Hosta. From the junction, follow the road south to the crossroads at NF 719 721. Turn right here and you are soon back at the starting point.

> **Hosta** (NF 725 723), the small hamlet near Tigh a' Ghearraidh, was the focus of an ongoing feud in the 14th and 15th centuries between two branches of the Clan Macdonald, Siol Murdoch and Siol Gorrie. Siol Murdoch inhabited the valley of Hosta, located downslope from a loch on the side of Cleitreabhal. It is said that under cover of darkness, members of Siol Gorrie came and dug away the soil embankment supporting this loch. The waters rushed down, flooded the valley and formed a new loch – the

present Loch Hosta. In this deluge, many of the people of Siol Murdoch perished. However, those who survived were not long in exacting a terrible revenge. They attacked Siol Gorrie, near the township of Udal (Walk 1.2). There was only one survivor; he first swam across to the nearby island of Orasaigh, and then fled south to find refuge in Lochboisdale.

WALK 1.13
Balranald Nature Reserve

Start/Finish	Visitor Centre (NF 707 707)
Distance	7km
Total Ascent	Negligible
Time	3–4hrs
Terrain	Machair and sandy coast
Maps	OS Explorer 454; OS Landranger 18
Access	Follow signs from the A865, 8km north-west of Clachan. The signs direct you to the visitor centre, open all year (NF 705 706).

Balranald is one of only two nature reserves designated by the RSPB in the Western Isles, and this area was chosen for its wide range of habitats and the associated diversity of wildlife. The walk described here adheres closely to the route recommended by the local visitor centre, and guided walks led by the RSPB warden are available at selected times in the spring and summer months (contact Jamie Boyle on 07768 042547). Although these months, with their numerous migratory birds and colourful display of wild flowers, are arguably the best time to visit the reserve, there is much to see throughout the year. A leaflet available at the visitor centre describes the contrasting seasonal attractions in detail.

The route itself is clearly marked by wooden posts, and the way first cuts across machair, before following the shore past dunes, rocky inlets and white sand beaches. Away from the effects of harmful pollutants, and coexisting in harmony with traditional crofting practices, these environments support a vast range of plant and animal species.

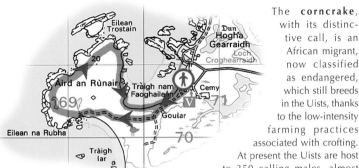

The **corncrake**, with its distinctive call, is an African migrant, now classified as endangered, which still breeds in the Uists, thanks to the low-intensity farming practices associated with crofting. At present the Uists are host to 350 calling males, almost 40% of the UK population. Corncrake walks are arranged by the RSPB between late May and early July.

Leave the visitor centre, heading south-west through a gate and along a farm track. Follow this track, clearly marked by posts, as it swings around to the west, first beside pasture and then alongside cultivated fields of oats, rye and barley. In May and June this section includes a high density of wild flowers. A detailed guidebook, to aid identification, may be useful. Both the casual observer and the dedicated botanist will enjoy trying to identify the numerous plant species, some familiar like poppies and wild pansies, but others rare, such as the frog orchid, seldom seen in other parts of the UK. Birds such as oystercatchers, ringed plovers and Greenland barnacle geese are also numerous on the machair.

As you near the shore, the track runs close by the dunes. At this point, it is worth making a short detour off the track to the left. The dune scenery is dramatic, showing clear evidence of erosion: the soft, largely unprotected sand an ongoing victim of the relentless savagery of the often-violent wind and waves. The remains of a fence line may be seen, some posts now barely 30cm tall, and becoming progressively shorter as dunes migrate

Looking west from Balranald to St Kilda

'CAPTAIN HOOK'

In 1965, a lone Grimsay fisherman, Ruairidh Eachainn Sheonaidh, was combing the beaches of Heisker when he happened upon an abandoned flare. Out of curiosity, he decided to set the flare alight. It exploded, destroying one of his hands and causing serious loss of blood. Despite managing to secure a tourniquet, he faced a desperate plight. Sea conditions were deteriorating and he knew there was no hope of rescue.

Returning to his boat, Ruairidh struggled to launch out into the heavy seas and somehow found the strength to navigate across six miles of open water, before making landfall near Hogha Gearraidh, just as darkness was approaching. Providentially, a local crofter had noticed the boat coming ashore and Ruairidh was rushed to hospital. He survived and was fitted with a metal hook. He returned to lobster fishing and was affectionately known as 'Captain Hook'.

inexorably inland. Over to the south-east, Heisker may easily be seen about 10km offshore. Although abandoned by humans in the 1950s, they are the breeding home to the second largest colony of Atlantic grey seals in the world.

On the beach beside the track you may see a variety of waders. Continue, crossing the fence at the designated point. The promontory beyond this fence, **Àird an Rùnair**, is the breeding area for a large number of ground-nesting birds, and a notice warns walkers not to stray off the marked path. ◄

The path is clear and easy to follow and veers north past a small loch and close to the rocky shoreline. In spring you may see skuas offshore, and in summer the loch is home to Arctic terns. The route carries on around the promontory, continually changing direction, north-east and then south, passing small coves and inlets fringed with tangle seaweed, and rounded boulders swept up by westerly storms.

Àird an Rùnair is the birthplace of the famous 18th-century Uist bard, John MacCodrum. He spent his last years near Loch a' Gheadais at the foot of Eabhal.

Wetland habitat at Balranald

After crossing the fence again, the path swings around to the north and follows the parabolic curve of **Tràigh nam Faoghailean**. The white sands contain a variety of shells, including small cowries, and in late summer the subtle blooms of sea rocket decorate the upper beach.

A leisurely stroll along the shore brings you back to your starting point at the visitor centre.

WALK 1.14
Baleshare (Baile Sear)

Start/Finish	Small car park beside the shore (NF 779 613)
Distance	7km
Total Ascent	Minimal
Time	3hrs
Terrain	Sandy coast
Maps	OS Explorer 454; OS Landranger 31

Baleshare is a small offshore island, connected to the mainland of North Uist by a causeway, constructed in 1962. The island is very flat and low-lying, and its position, bordering the Atlantic, makes it particularly vulnerable to erosion by wind and waves. In fact, the Gaelic name for Baleshare, Baile Sear, translates as 'East Town'. Baile Siar, the western part of the former island, disappeared beneath the Atlantic waves many centuries ago. The beach along the west side of Baleshare, being so exposed, is a great place for an invigorating walk or run. There is plenty of interest, as the topography of the coastline is constantly changing, and it sometimes reveals unexpected treasures. Back in 2005, a severe storm temporarily exposed the site of a roundhouse dating from the Iron Age.

The beach stretches over 7km, if you include the long spit at the northern end of the island. Dedicated beachcombers may wish to tackle the whole, but a smaller section, described here, is ideal for a morning or afternoon outing. It is probably more enjoyable at low tide when a vast expanse of sand is exposed, and the surface is firm. However, keep an eye out for the tide coming in – it moves very rapidly.

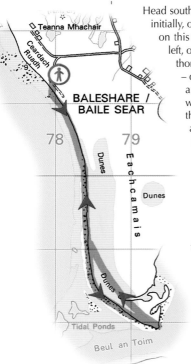

Head south from the car park. Either follow a track initially, or just go straight to the beach. Navigation on this walk is not a problem: shingle to your left, ocean to your right, and sand, your natural thoroughfare, stretching far into the distance – due south towards the noonday sun. After a few hundred metres the shingle gives way to sand dunes, and it is easy to see the marks of the wind. The marram does an amazing job at stabilisation, but once the dune base is undercut, collapse and retreat soon follow.

Towards the southern end of the beach, as you approach Benbecula, shingle takes over again and here there is even more evidence of marine power. The upper beach is littered with battered lobster creels, ripped from their moorings out in the Atlantic. The shore now curves round in a south-easterly direction, and Benbecula looks tantalisingly close. Beware! The water flowing through the dividing channel is deep and fast flowing.

As you proceed along the base of the dunes, you will notice **blow-outs**, deep sand gullies, perpendicular to the main dune ridge. These lines of weakness have been exploited and enlarged by frequent south-westerly gales. Fences with mesh to trap the sand have been constructed in some areas, but it is difficult to contain the relentless force of the elements.

The outward beach walk soon terminates, as water blocks any further onward progress (NF 792 580). However, the highest dune in the area is only 50m inland, and it is definitely worth the climb.

Erosion in the dune ridge

From its top, the **view** is both interesting and surprising. To the south you can survey much of Benbecula and nearby Balivanich, with its landmark water tower. East lies the North Ford, with Eabhal rising in the distance, and out west the Atlantic, with Heisker not far offshore. However, looking north to Eachcamais, the landscape is strange – an almost endless, corrugated terrain of dunes, but now green, transformed into pasture.

Having scaled the dune ridge, it is worth following its crest for the start of the return journey, but avoid the very edge, in case of collapse. The ridge arches and twists like an Alpine arête, and for those wearing shorts, the deep, spiky marram helps to maintain a sharp

Marram grass with Eabhal in the background

focus. After a while, descend once more to the beach and its smooth, stable surface. Now simply head north, and about 3km up the coast, a prominent fence post warns you that your inland detour back to the car park is imminent.

2 BENBECULA
Beinn na Faoghla

Harvest time on the machair

INTRODUCTION

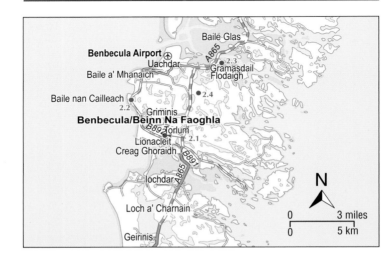

The Isle of Benbecula lies between North and South Uist and since 1960 has been connected to its neighbours by a series of bridges and causeways. The island is generally flat, but resembles its larger neighbours in having contrasting topography between its east and west coasts, moorland and machair.

The walks described in this section not only sample the different landscapes and habitats, but also visit various sites of historical

significance, particularly in relation to Bonnie Prince Charlie, who stayed on the island before being transported to Skye, following his escape from Culloden in 1746.

The main road, the A865, crosses the centre of Benbecula on its way between the two Uists. However, the equally important secondary route, the B892, links to the more densely populated west coast. Balivanich is the main service centre and is home to the island's airport.

WALK 2.1
Borgh

Start/Finish	Car park at Sgoil Lionacleit (NF 781 499)
Distance	8km
Total Ascent	Negligible
Time	3–4hrs
Terrain	Machair and sandy coast
Maps	OS Explorer 453; OS Landranger 22

This route visits Benbecula's beach and machair environments, and also passes close to the remains of Teampull Bhuirgh and Caisteal Bhuirgh. In spring and summer, the machair section is adorned with a colourful selection of wild flowers. Numerous bird species may be identified en route, and otters are also known to frequent the area. Although some of the walking is along roads, these are generally very quiet, with only occasional traffic.

The route starts and finishes at Sgoil Lionacleit. Refreshments may be available here, and there is also a swimming pool with other sports facilities.

Caisteal Bhuirgh

Head north-west from the school exit and turn right almost immediately, just before the caravan site. Follow the road to the end of the tarmac and continue along a track across pasture, passing through two gates, before joining the Torlum road. Take the road east for a short distance to where a footpath sign to Griminis steers

Irish Lady's-tresses Orchid

The machair is a flat, low-lying coastal plain formed by sand blowing inland from the shore. Machair soils are relatively fertile and alkaline due to high shell content.

you north, beside the old **Torlum schoolhouse**. A track, marked on the OS map, leads north to intercept the Griminis road near a transmission mast. Now head west along the road to the junction at NF 766 518. Although the landscape along this section may appear rather flat and uninspiring, the surrounding marshy habitats provide good opportunities for sighting a range of birds including, in summer, the red necked phalarope. The rare Irish Lady's-tresses Orchid may also be seen.

On reaching the junction with the main road to Balivanich, you are opposite a large shed. Go round the right side of this building, across the dunes and down to the beach. The route now turns south, following the shore for almost 2km. This is a splendid place, almost completely deserted, but with a real chance of seeing otters scampering seawards across the sand. At low tide there is a vast expanse of sand to enjoy, and, on a clear day, there are enticing views towards the distant hills, The Three Peaks of South Uist (Walk 3.4). The upper beach is often covered by deep accumulations of tangle seaweed, harvested in the past to be processed into kelp.

Just before the promontory at the southern end of the beach near **Sìdhean Bhuirgh**, a track leads inland through a gate, which gives access to the machair. ◄

The track continues across this natural grassland with its seasonal splashes of floral colour. On the way you pass close to an obvious mound, the remains of **Teampull Bhuirgh**, an important archaeological site where excavation is ongoing. The track reaches the road close to **Caisteal Bhuirgh** (NF 774 505), a castle dating from the 14th century. From here, head south-west along the road back to Sgoil Lionacleit.

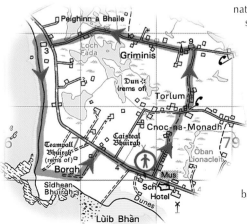

WALK 2.2
Culla Bay

Start/Finish	Car park beside Nunton Steadings (NF 765 536)
Distance	2.5km
Total Ascent	Minimal
Time	1–2hrs
Terrain	Sandy coast
Maps	OS Explorer 453; OS Landranger 22

This is a short, low-level walk, ideal for a morning, afternoon or summer evening. The route follows the beach and dunes at Culla Bay, but also passes sites of historical interest.

From the car park, follow the road south-west for 300m to a passing place, where a double gate on the right allows access to the shore. A track leads through a break in the dunes down to the beach at **Culla**. Go north around the curving sweep of the bay, adjusting your line according to the state of the tide. If the tide is high, leave the sand about halfway along the bay and then follow the dune

Culla Bay

ridge. However, at low tide, continue along the shore to the end of the beach. In either event, you should reach a car park/picnic site at NF 763 543. From this point, a path, marked on the OS map, leads back to the road again.

> The short walk back to Nunton Steadings passes a **burial ground** and a ruined Chapel, St Mary's, built in medieval times. Further on is Nunton House, the former Clanranald residence. Flora MacDonald left from Nunton when she masterminded the escape of Bonnie Prince Charlie, The Young Pretender. The Prince, disguised as a maid, was escorted to Ròisinis in eastern Benbecula (Walk 2.3), before crossing the Minch to Skye.

Another footpath is shown on the OS map leaving Nunton (**Baile nan Cailleach**) in a south-easterly direction. In theory, this path should take you easily across to the Griminis road, but in practice, the latter part of this route is very wet and blocked by a fence. However, for those with an interest in ornithology or botany, it is worth going as far as the bridge at NF 775 527. You are sure to encounter numerous wetland plants and bird species. After this sortie into the interior of Benbecula, it is wise to retreat once more to Nunton.

WALK 2.3
Ròisinis

Start/Finish	Start of the unfenced section of the Caolas Fhlodaigh road, about 400m beyond the thatched cottage (NF 831 553)
Distance	13km
Total Ascent	200m
Time	5–6hrs
Terrain	Moor
Maps	OS Explorer 453; OS Landranger 22

The walk out to Ròisinis visits the remote area in the extreme north-eastern corner of Benbecula. It follows part of the route taken by Bonnie Prince Charlie on his escape to Skye. The walk starts from the Caolas Fhlodaigh road, just south of the causeway to Grimsay and North Uist. This approach initially crosses heather moorland instead of following a path, but it is shorter than the normal route from Market Stance (Stansa na Fèille) and probably more scenic. In the summer months you may encounter a rich variety of flora, well adapted to these acidic, peaty soils: Tormentil, Bog Aspodel, Heath Spotted Orchid, among others.

Although there is a good track for much of the way, the ground is poorly drained and even the path becomes waterlogged. Stout, waterproof footwear is recommended, as well as a compass, or GPS, for navigating across the moor.

Leave the road just west of the lochan (NF 832 553) and head across the moor in a south-south-easterly direction. After surmounting an initial rise, a ruined shieling should become visible in the distance, along the same bearing. Proceed to the **shieling** (NF 824 544) as directly as possible, but minor detours may be needed to avoid the boggier sections. Now follow a path away from the shieling, but still heading south-south-east. As this path fades, continue around the left (east) side of the lochs ahead and, after a short climb, a small gate gives access to the main track heading east from Stansa na Fèille (NF 840 535).

The shieling at NF 824 544

The route is now straightforward for a while, as the track passes through two gates and over a small hill, before dropping to a very flat area before a third gate. The ground here is often very wet, and it may be necessary to find a drier alternative on slightly higher ground to the right. Go through the gate, and after approximately 200m you pass a derelict concrete foundation on your left (NF 855 533). Just beyond this structure, a narrow path forks right towards some shielings beside the shore; these are worth exploring, if time allows, but the way to Ròisinis follows the main track, straight ahead. The track remains clear and good for a short distance, but it soon narrows and veers right past a narrow lochan. Beware of a short, sharp drop down to the water! A broader section of path leads to a final gate.

From here on, it is often hard to identify the most efficient route, as there are several paths, and some quickly peter out. However, the general direction is east-north-east, towards the summit of Beinn Rodagraich on the island of Ronay (NF 893 546). One of the more obvious paths passes close to the shore beside an inlet on the southern side of the headland. This locality seems to trap all manner of sea-borne detritus. In addition to the knee-deep accumulation of bladder wrack seaweed, there are assorted floats and, sadly, an abundance of less attractive jetsam. After the shore, you rise back to an area of almost featureless moorland, and it is advisable to keep checking your bearings, either by compass or by focusing on the Beinn. However, although the moor appears almost endless, progress is encouragingly rapid, and you soon reach the northern end of a loch with two obvious small trees and a solitary marker post (NF 867 535). ▸

Looking east, you now see an area of green pasture and, surprisingly, for the east side of Benbecula, sand dunes. Cross the final stretch of moor to this oasis of fertility. There is also a **building** (NF 873 536), now derelict, but inhabited until the 1960s. It seems so remote in this age of the car, but at that time, with the sea the main thoroughfare, access was rarely a problem. There is a small sandy bay, with views across to nearby Grimsay, a good place to relax before the return journey.

Bonnie Prince Charlie set sail for Skye from eastern Benbecula. Some believe that he left from a point just south-east of Ròisinis at NF 876 531. However, recent research suggests that, after hearing that enemy forces were fast approaching, he moved further south before embarking from the southern shores of Loch Uisgeabhagh.

Caolas Fhlodaigh

ng Stone

Shielings

Loch na Bèire

Loch na Deighe fo Thuath

Shieling

Loch an Tairbh

Shieling

Bàgh na Muice

Ròisinis

Dunes

93

The way back essentially retraces the outward route, but the initial section is somewhat puzzling. The bearing is now west-south-west, and if you like something to aim for, target a line halfway between Ruabhal, Benbecula's highest point, and the distant windmill at Lionacleit (NF 783 497). Once across the moor and past the inlet, you regain the path, with easier walking for the next 2km. However, study the map carefully and remain alert to ensure that you do leave the track via the gate at NF 840 535.

The direction from here is north-west, past the lochs and then to the shieling at NF 824 544. On the final stretch over the moor, you may derive encouragement from the knowledge that the buildings of Caolas Fhlodaigh really are getting closer!

WALK 2.4
Ruabhal

Start/Finish	Parking place near the end of the surfaced road, just before a cattle grid (NF 811 535)
Distance	4km
Total Ascent	120m
Time	2hrs
Terrain	Hill and moor
Maps	OS Explorer 453; OS Landranger 22
Access	Head east from the crossroads at Stansa na Fèille (NF 805 536).

Ruabhal, the only hill in Benbecula, is an excellent vantage point, despite its modest stature. The return trip to Ruabhal, which may be completed comfortably in under 2hrs, is a great way to stretch the legs, and there is a clear path to follow all the way. Please don't be deterred by the approach drive!

Leave the parking place, heading over the cattle grid and along the track in an easterly direction. After passing through an open gate, the track continues close to the shore of **Loch Bà Una**. Carry on until a path, identified by a marker post, forks off to the left, just before a small quarry. Follow this path, initially over boggy ground, but then up and across dry, open hillside to reach the corner of the fence. The path splits at this point, but either option is fine – the only way is up! Soon, after a final steeper section, the ground levels off and the trig point comes into view.

View towards Ruabhal, Benbecula's highest point

From the top of **Ruabhal**, the broad expanse of moor and water is revealed down below, and above are the vast skies with their infinite cloud patterns: ephemeral

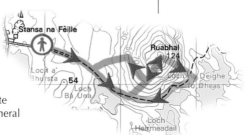

THE SHIELING OF THE SINGLE NIGHT

In the area to the south-west of Ruabhal are the ruins of a shieling known as Àiridh na h-Aon Oidhche (NF 817 524) (Explorer map), which translates as 'the Shieling of the Single Night'. Locals tell of sinister happenings which occurred there long ago.

A shepherd and his two sons were at the shieling with their dog, attending to the sheep. As evening fell, the talk came round to their wish for the company of females. There was a knock at the door and in came three beautiful women. The father stayed in the main room with one of the women while his sons went to the next room with the other two. As the father sat there, he noticed in horror that the woman he was with was beginning to grow a beak. Then, to his dismay, as he looked towards the next room, he saw blood seeping from under the door. Terrified, he made an excuse to go outside and made his escape, followed by the dog. The woman soon realised that he had gone and gave chase, closing in on the fleeing man. In desperation, he called on the dog to attack the woman while he continued on his flight. Once home, he filled three pails of milk, leaving them outside the house to quench the dog's now insatiable thirst. The following morning, the dog was dead on the doorstep, but without a single hair on its body. The sons were later found murdered, and the shieling was forever abandoned. It is said that, to this day, even livestock avoid the area.

and ever changing. North and south lie the fords, now spanned by their causeways, and more distant, the hills: Eabhal, Thacla and Beinn Mhòr.

For the route down there is a minor variation, if desired. Descend as far as the fence corner, but then follow the fence line beside the reseeded pasture, before cutting across heather to rejoin the main track. This option is slightly shorter and the going is generally fine. However, after heavy rain it might be a bit boggy at the foot of the hill.

If you wish to extend the walk, descend the more rugged eastern slopes of Ruabhal. After a short, steep descent, you regain the track which meanders around the base of the hill back to the starting point.

3 SOUTH UIST
Uibhist a Deas

Beinn Mhòr's summit arête

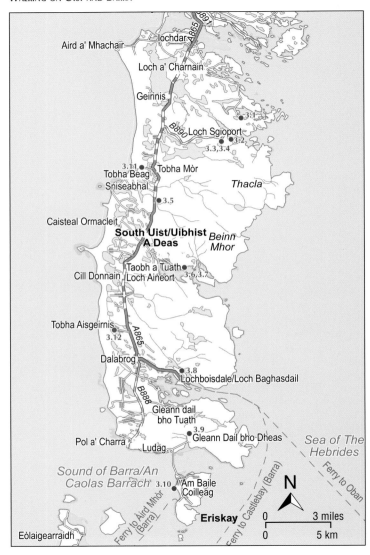

INTRODUCTION

Eriskay from Marabhal's cairned summit (Walk 3.9)

South Uist, the largest island of the southern archipelago, stretches almost 40km between Benbecula and Eriskay. The island has a clear east-west divide: the rugged hills and rocky inlets of the east side contrasting with the flat coastal machair and sandy shoreline of the west. The walks chosen for South Uist reflect these differences.

The main road, the A865, almost bisects the island, providing a neat boundary between moorland and machair. Minor offshoots from this arterial route access the sea lochs: Loch Sgioport and Loch Aineort, the starting points for walks to Beinn Mhòr, Thacla and The Three Peaks (Walks 3.6, 3.3, 3.4).

Lochboisdale, the main village on South Uist, is also the embarkation point for ferries to Oban and Castlebay.

WALK 3.1

Loch Sgioport

Start/Finish	End of the Loch a' Chàrnain road (NF 835 402)
Distance	7km; 5km for shorter option
Total Ascent	200m
Time	3–4hrs
Terrain	Moor
Maps	OS Explorer 453; OS Landranger 22
Access	Follow the road to Loch a' Chàrnain from the junction 2km south of the South Uist causeway. Travel south-east, past the power station and assorted fish farming sites, to the very end of the road.

This walk enters a remote, seldom-visited area in the north-eastern part of South Uist. This part of the island was reasonably well populated in the past, the scattered ruins bearing testimony to a more extensive, once thriving, community. The route combines some well-defined tracks with other areas of open moorland. Bird life is plentiful, with abundant species from both coastal and moorland habitats.

From the turning space at the road end, follow the obvious track to the left of the houses, heading south-south-east. Pass through a gate, and then, after a further 100m, bear left at the junction (NF 836 399). The route now goes roughly east along a good, dry path, undoubtedly well used in bygone days.

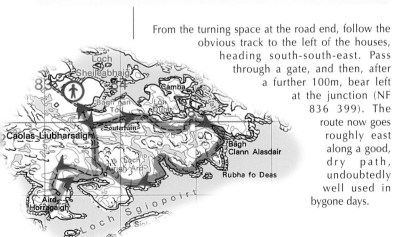

Across this apparently inhospitable heather moor, careful scrutiny provides surprising evidence of a once well-cultivated **crofting landscape**. Geometrical patterns in the undulating terrain indicate the parallel lines of former lazy beds, perhaps used for the potato crops. Broad views open up east to Skye, and north across Benbecula to the distinctive profile of Eabhal in North Uist.

The track ends beside a narrow inlet, the way further east blocked by a fence (NF 851 400). You must now take to the pathless moor, heading west-south-west towards the next destination, an old house at NF 838 393. It is best to go south initially towards **Rubha fo Deas**, where you catch a glimpse of distant Uisinis lighthouse (Walk 3.2). As you follow the coast westwards, you are occasionally forced inland around bays, and then back to the shore where lochs block the direct way ahead. It is important to note that at most tides a passage is possible where Loch Àirigh Àrd meets the sea (NF 843 392). However, the rocks by the shore are slippery. For most of the way the walking is good and the ground is surprisingly dry. ▶

Along the coast there are numerous sea birds, and swans seem to delight in the undisturbed tranquility of the sheltered lochans.

The abandoned pier at Loch Sgioport

A line of cliffs forces you inland from the bay at NF 842 392, along the fence line in a north-westerly direction. Over the rise ahead, you pass an **old house** (NF 838 393) before joining a path.

There are now two options. The path to the **right** takes you comfortably back to your starting point, about 1km to the north. However, if you wish to extend the walk, you may follow the path to the **left**. Passing through two gates, the path swings right, beside an extensive area of ruins. Continue west for about 500m, but then veer south beneath a small cliff topped by another ruin. A vague path continues to a more recently abandoned dwelling at NF 832 390. It is worth going on a bit further to climb a small hillock with a rocky knoll, **Àird Horragaigh**.

> The view south is impressive and thought provoking. In the distance lies **Thacla** with its brooding northern corries. However, nearer at hand, just across Loch Sgioport, is the **decaying pier**, a flourishing hive of activity in bygone days. This sheltered sea loch was, until the 1950s, an important harbour for South Uist.

After absorbing the view, return to the abandoned dwelling and then retrace your steps to the gates for the way home. To save a little time and distance, it is possible to cut across from the abandoned dwelling, closer to the shore. However, the ground is wet and boggy in places.

WALK 3.2
Uisinis lighthouse and Nicolson's Leap

Start/Finish	Small car park near the eastern end of the road to Loch Sgioport (NF 827 386)
Distance	17km
Total Ascent	500m
Time	6–8hrs
Terrain	Moor and rocky coast
Maps	OS Explorer 453; OS Landranger 22

This walk combines two notable landmarks on the east coast of South Uist: Uisinis lighthouse, perched on top of a cliff overlooking the Little Minch, and Nicolson's Leap, a deep chasm separating a sea stack from the main island.

The walk takes you through some of the wildest, most remote country in the Uists – an area favoured by deer, and those stalking them. Although the Total Ascent is relatively small, the way is constantly challenging, and navigation is far from straightforward. The route crosses rough moorland with only faint tracks, and much of the ground is wet and boggy for most of the year. However, for those seeking peace and solitude in harmony with nature, this walk is ideal.

It is best to avoid this area in the main deerstalking season from October to December. If in doubt, contact Stòras Uibhist (tel. 01878 700101).

Go west for a short distance from the car park and you will see a signed footpath to Caolas Mòr and Thacla. Proceed along this path, winding past old ruins above the shore. Shortly after crossing a second wooden bridge, you will see a faint track heading off right, up the hillside, behind an old croft house. Follow this track, the route taken by stalkers in the shooting season. The climb is steep at first but then levels off, and you are soon heading east past a long, narrow lochan and across an old fence line. The track does tend to

Map continued on page 104

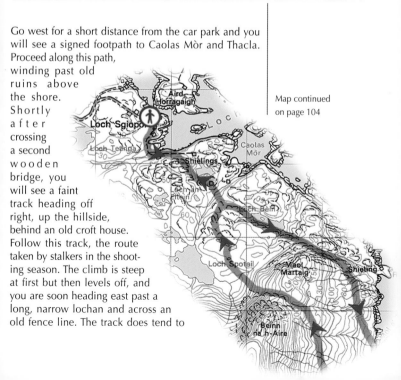

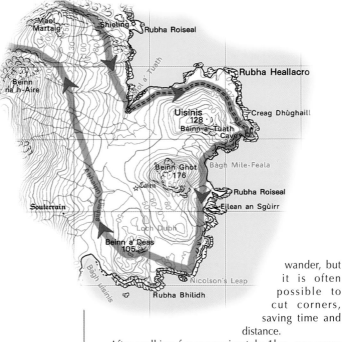

wander, but it is often possible to cut corners, saving time and distance.

After walking for approximately 1km, you cross the burn flowing north from Loch Spotail (NF 835 374). Once over the burn, follow the track along the bank for a short distance north, and then ascend the hillside heading east until **Loch Bèin**, with its small islet, comes into view. Beyond the loch there is an obvious gap in Thacla's north ridge: your next target. You now have to abandon your trusted man-made track, and, as long as the gap remains your focus, there are a number of options: the choice is yours. The easiest route bypasses Loch Bèin on its south side, and then contours round to reach the gap (NF 849 369). Now the fun starts. Once through the gap, a distant headland, **Rubha Hallacro**, becomes visible to the south-east. With this as your new target, make your way along the side of a heathery valley. New tracks do appear, but surely not the work of a mere human. The heather is deep, and seriously large strides are needed to make effective onward progress. However, the going eases after 400m, and the route now makes a gradually descending traverse in a south-south-easterly direction to meet the coast beside a small bay, **Mol a' Tuath** (NF 857 355). This section provides comfortable walking, and has straightforward navigation, apart from short detours across valleys draining east to the sea.

Once at the shore, head a short distance inland, past an old **building**, to intercept a track, the access route for the lighthouse. The way ahead is now obvious, and on a clear day there is ample time to admire views of Skye's Duirinish coastline. After a pleasant stroll, with the luxury of a well-defined track to guide you, you come upon the **lighthouse**, surrounded by a walled enclosure.

It is easy to see why this site was chosen for **Uisinis lighthouse**. Nestling on a rocky headland 50m above the waves, it commands outstanding views across the sea over a huge arc. Uisinis, like so many of Scotland's spectacular lighthouses, was designed by members of the Stevenson family. It was completed in 1857. The area around the lighthouse is worth a brief exploration, but these cliffs, like many

Uisinis lighthouse on its rocky headland

in the region, have a convex profile, steepening downwards, and merit serious respect. It is also worth noting that the cave marked on the OS map is not visible from the land.

From the lighthouse, the way now goes south-south-west, but unfortunately not in a straight line. Major diversions inland are essential, as the coastline is indented, with precipitous cliffs and steep-sided inlets. Occasionally, it is necessary to drop almost to sea level, but this is not a serious problem. You will find small, sheltered bays, ideal for a picnic stop.

The land rises again as you approach **Nicolson's Leap**, but proceed with care: the sea stack appears unexpectedly. Suddenly, before you, there is a deep cleft separating the cliff from the pinnacle offshore.

A local tale tells how **Nicolson's Leap** got its name. A legendary character, after an affair with the clan chief's wife, was hotly pursued across the moors. Reaching the edge of the precipitous cliff, he leapt across the chasm, somehow grasping the adjacent

Nicolson's Leap

rocky pinnacle. Sadly, unable to escape from this temporary refuge, he is believed to have perished on the stack.

The way back to the start follows the clifftop west, and you are soon able to look back to gain a better view of the Leap and appreciate the enormity of the feat. Now head inland, north-west towards **Beinn a' Deas**. On the face ahead you will notice a green patch of grass beneath a rocky overhang, the entrance to a cave. If you are able to negotiate the narrow opening, a small hideaway is revealed inside: perhaps another refuge of Bonnie Prince Charlie.

Leaving the cave, trend left and over the rise ahead. The way ahead should be clearly visible: north-west across a flat plain and then up the opposite slope to engage a stalker's track snaking diagonally up the hillside. This track is a continuation of the familiar trail from earlier in the walk, and it should be a helpful guide for what still remains of the route. The track continues in a north-westerly direction, crossing Thacla's north ridge over an obvious pass (NF 845 362). As you summit the ridge, the view west provides added impetus for the homeward journey: Loch Spotail immediately at your feet, and Loch Druidibeag beyond, stretching west to the machair.

The walk now descends steeply, before crossing the expanse of wet moorland north of **Loch Spotail**. There are occasional cairns and wooden ramps to reassure you of the correct route, but, if in doubt, use Ben Tairbert (NF 807 395) as a direction indicator. The terrain is mixed: in some areas, smooth, bare rock – a natural, firm pavement – but elsewhere the track crosses blanket bog, a squelchy morasse of sphagnum and cotton grass. At length, the track drops once again to ford the burn north of Loch Spotail. Now retrace your steps, still north-west, back to the gravel path, and onwards to the car park.

WALK 3.3

The Northern Corries of Thacla

Start/Finish	Sharp left-hand bend on the Loch Sgioport (Skipport) road (NF 818 386)
Distance	13km
Total Ascent	700m
Time	5–6hrs
Terrain	Hill and moor
Maps	OS Explorer 453; OS Landranger 22
Access	Head east from the crossroads near Groigearraidh (NF 774 397).

This walk, which visits Thacla's two north-facing corries, Coire Ruadall and Coire na h-Eitich, includes an amazing variety of landscapes: glaciated upland, steep-sided ravines, lochs and waterfalls. However, the walk is relatively long and strenuous, and the absence of paths can make route finding difficult, particularly in misty conditions. Some of the moorland areas are boggy, and unwary walkers may find themselves sinking to waist level or even deeper in pockets of mire.

Water-loving plant species are prolific across the undulating marshy approach, but in the secluded, sheltered ravines there is a profusion of ferns and wild flowers. Deer are relatively common in the upper corries, and the mountain and moorland habitats are attractive to birds of prey, including golden eagle.

Shetland ponies are often in close attendance beside the road at the start of the walk. They are cute, yet very persistent, and may make exiting your car with a packed lunch intact the most challenging part of the day!

From the starting point, head south-east along the northern shore of **Loch Teanga**. At the end of the loch turn south and continue over a small hill to cross a narrow burn at NF 820 380. The route continues due south, but if visibility is good, the summit of Thacla provides a helpful direction indicator. However, it may be necessary to make minor diversions around a number of small lochans and areas of abundant green sphagnum moss. There is also a

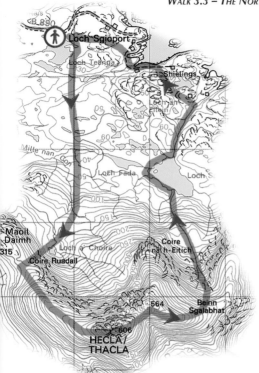

slightly awkward river crossing at NF 820 370 – the water is deeper than it looks.

After this crossing, Coire Ruadall lies clearly ahead to the south, up a gradual incline. The ravine at NF 830 362 is certainly worth a detour and can be accessed either by closely following the river upstream or by an easy scramble down the eastern bank. A short passage across partly submerged boulders takes you to the edge of a deep plunge pool at the foot of two small converging waterfalls. This is an idyllic place: a tranquil and secluded garden, especially in springtime and early summer when it is clothed with abundant foliage.

The ravine may be exited by an unlikely looking scramble up the left-hand waterfall to half height, followed by a traverse right, along a bramble-covered ledge. However, this is not recommended when the stream is in spate, and it is almost as quick to retrace your steps downstream for a short distance.

The route now continues south-west over grass and heathery slopes to reach the floor of **Coire Ruadall** and its glacial tarn, **Loch a' Choire**. There are several options from here. The direct route to the summit of Thacla, although quicker, is a tedious grind, bereft of scenic quality. Probably better all round is to skirt the west side of the lochan and then climb steeply up the corrie backwall to reach the shoulder on the western ridge of **Thacla** (NF 813 355). The benefit of this choice is the superb view which appears as the ridge is attained: Beinn Mhòr directly south, with the coastal machair and white sands of the Atlantic shoreline towards the south-west.

Thacla's vertiginous summit

The climb continues south-east along the broad ridge towards Thacla's summit, relatively steep at first, but then

flattening out – excellent walking terrain. The final section steepens again and you will have to thread a way between a number of rocky outcrops. The summit itself is in a superb position, on a rocky knoll with precipitous slopes dropping to the south and east. ▸

The route leaves Thacla's main summit, heading north-east, and gentle walking on broad, grassy slopes leads quickly to a secondary summit at NF 830 349. Now turn east, descending towards **Beinn Sgalabhat**, and then gradually veer north into **Coire na h-Eitich**.

A burn drains north-north-west out of the corrie into another ravine with waterfalls. It is safer to descend well to the west of the watercourse to avoid dangerous overhangs above the steep sides of the ravine. Once the gradient lessens, it is possible to scramble down to the river, and a further scramble back upstream provides access to the waterfalls.

Return downstream and now continue around the shore of **Loch Spotail** until you reach the point where a river drains northwards at NF 833 369. Follow the eastern bank for approximately 750m to where a track cuts across the river. This track, although somewhat circuitous, and indistinct in places, leads you north-west and back to your starting point.

The view now encompasses both coasts of South Uist, the Little Minch and Skye to the east and, on a clear day, Heisker and St Kilda visible to the north-west.

WALK 3.4
The Three Peaks

Start	Start from the Loch Sgioport road, near the sharp bend (NF 818 386)
Finish	Taobh a Tuath Loch Aineort road end (NF 788 283), or Sniseabhal (NF 768 346)
Distance	16km to Taobh a Tuath; 17km to Sniseabhal
Total Ascent	1300m
Time	5–7hrs
Terrain	Hill
Maps	OS Explorer 453; OS Landranger 22

The Three Peaks of South Uist – Thacla, Beinn Mhòr and Beinn Choradail – although less well known than some more illustrious trios, nevertheless provide an excellent excursion, and present the hillwalker with a good opportunity to climb the more isolated peak of Beinn Chorodail. Although quite difficult logistically, because a second car or taxi is required at the finish point, it is desirable to complete a linear traverse of the hills. The route described here starts in the north from the road to Loch Sgioport, and finishes at Taobh a Tuath Loch Aineort. Although it is possible to do the traverse from south to north, the north to south route is arguably preferable, because the ascents of Thacla and Beinn Mhòr are more gradual, and the walk in this direction also provides superb views into Beinn Mhòr's shady northern corrie. An alternative finish at Sniseabhal is also an option.

Apart from the great walking, which is largely on dry, open hillsides, there are great opportunities to see both deer and golden eagle.

It is important to note that some of the route finding is awkward and confusing, so it is wise to choose a clear day for this outing.

Thacla

From the starting point at the roadside, head south-east along the northern shore of **Loch Teanga**. At the end of this loch strike south, and then make a gradual ascent of the hillside ahead before descending to cross the narrow burn at NF 820 380. From here there are different options. Either follow the route described for Walk 3.3 The Northern Corries of Thacla, or opt for a more direct variation. In the latter case, you must next head for the western end of **Loch Fada** on a south-south-easterly bearing. En route, some of the ground is boggy, but it should be possible to navigate a reasonably dry passage. You may also encounter small lochans on the way, although none should necessitate a major detour. After walking for just over 1km across the moor, make a short descent to the end of Loch Fada (NF 823 369). There are some conveniently placed stepping-stones for the crossing.

The slopes of **Thacla** are now ahead. They start off gently, but gradually the gradient increases as you begin to enter the corrie. As you climb, you may pass unusual detached boulders, possibly glacial erratics, transported

Map continued
on page 115

by ice and deposited here at the end of the Ice Age. After a moderate ascent of approximately 1.5km, the heathery slopes are replaced by the grass and rock of the steep corrie side. Although some of the terrain appears forbidding, at about half height there is a terrace that provides comfortable walking beneath cliffs and gullies. At length, the terrace intersects with a large grassy gully cleaving the corrie face. Follow this gully left up steep grass until you reach the saddle between Thacla's peaks (NF 829 348). The view opens up eastward, down to the coast and then to the Inner Hebrides further distant. Now turn south-west for the final section, mainly on gently angled grass slopes, reminiscent of the northern fells of Lakeland. An enjoyable stroll takes you to Thacla's airy summit, an ideal place from which to study peak number two, **Beinn Choradail**.

The best descent route off Thacla, if you wish to avoid the coarse scree, is initially in a westerly direction along the short summit ridge, and then down a small rocky gully. As the ground levels off, bear left over mixed ground for approximately 50m until grass is predominant. Gradually descend the grassy slopes diagonally, now in a south-westerly direction, until an open gully cuts back left, beside steep, rocky slabs. You now reach a more gentle section, once more sloping south-west, down to the bealach, the watershed between east and

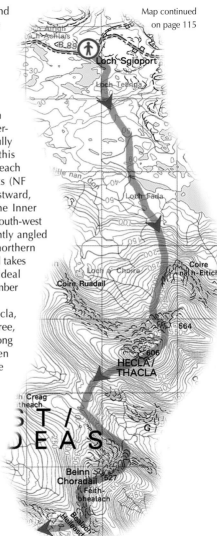

west. As you cross this broad saddle, heading south towards your next hill, the view south-east is especially appealing – Gleann Uisinis framing distant Rùm. The terrain is mixed, grass and heather interspersed with large outcrops of gneiss, plucked and abraded by glacial forces. Small cliffs may block your way and create the occasional cul de sac, but these just serve to focus the concentration. Along the way, you may also pass small lochans, potentially attractive, but black and uninviting even on the warmest day.

As you draw closer to Beinn Chorodail, the final rocky buttress rears up ahead. Unless you are equipped for some serious rock climbing, you must choose between one of two alternative routes, left or right. Choosing the former, you first ascend a series of small grassy terraces and then continue left along the base of the cliff. In due course you will cross a narrow eroded gully. From the far side of this gully, climb a short but steep grassy slope, before cutting back right to the top. The right-hand option takes you up mixed ground beneath the steep chimney on Chorodail's west face. Moving right from the foot of the chimney, you will find a much easier gully, and a short scramble

Gleann Uisinis and Loch Corodail

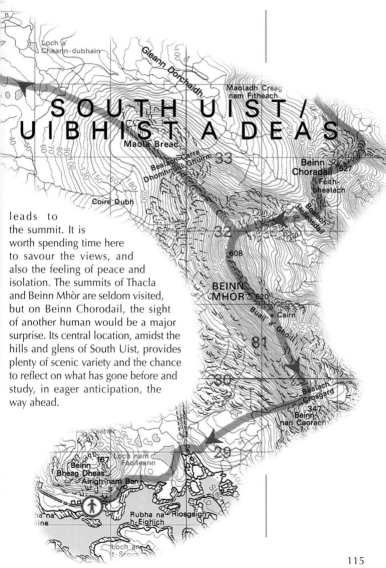

leads to the summit. It is worth spending time here to savour the views, and also the feeling of peace and isolation. The summits of Thacla and Beinn Mhòr are seldom visited, but on Beinn Chorodail, the sight of another human would be a major surprise. Its central location, amidst the hills and glens of South Uist, provides plenty of scenic variety and the chance to reflect on what has gone before and study, in eager anticipation, the way ahead.

Loch Heileasdail and Beinn Mhòr's northern corrie

Beinn Mhòr

The route to **Bealach Heileasdail**, the next stage of the walk, is in a south-south-westerly direction, but some of the ground is steep and rocky, and requires care, particularly in bad weather. After the initial moderate descent from the summit, work your way across and down the western slope of the hill on a gradually descending traverse. The grassy slope eventually terminates beside a rocky buttress. Vague, eroded sheep tracks lead downwards. Follow these to the base of the cliff, and then descend directly over mixed ground to Bealach Heileasdal (NF 816 323). This low point, before the ascent to Beinn Mhòr, allows fine views in almost all directions, but the outlook to the south and east demands your closest attention. Gleann Heileasdal opens up to the south-east, cradling its loch of constantly changing blues, and south lies Beinn Mhòr's corrie, its north-facing aspect almost devoid of sunshine. The sombre mood is reinforced by an amphitheatre of steep, dark cliffs falling directly from the summit, and precipices, grotesquely slashed by deep, slanting gullies.

The onward route to the top essentially follows the western the rim of the corrie. Cross the Bealach via an undulating area of grass and rock, passing an old fence line on the way. Ahead lies **Beinn Mhòr's** north-east ridge. Although the climb is substantial, about 300m, there is plenty of variety, and the ascent appears to pass without too much fatigue. The easiest line lies slightly to the left, up a series of open, grassy gullies, but, if preferred, scrambling is available on outcrops further right. The ridge eventually merges into a broad, flat shoulder, and the junction with the north-west ridge. Now veer south, up a moderate slope, to reach the north-west top.

To reach the main summit, you may follow the crest the whole way, but this will involve short pitches of scrambling. To avoid using your hands, it is necessary to switch from side to side. For the first 400m either flank is suitable. However, as you proceed, small cliffs appear on the right (south-western) side, and the easiest route follows the left side, about 20m below the crest. A further 200m onwards, return briefly to the crest before following an obvious path, now on the right side of the ridge. This path does lead you to the summit plateau, but be careful – it is easy to end up at another subsidiary summit. As you initially emerge on to the plateau where the ground flattens out, be sure to cut back, sharp left, to locate a trig point surrounded by a stone shelter; this is the true summit of **Beinn Mhòr**. Avoid straying north of the trig point – the ground falls precipitously to the corrie floor.

Descent to Taobh a Tuath Loch Aineort

The summit area broadens towards the south-east, and the route now crosses this grassy plateau to reach a secondary summit with a large cairn. Continue in a south-south-easterly direction. The surface is grassy but the ridge gradually narrows and steepens – good walking, but sometimes slippery after rain. The descent is surprisingly rapid and, about 1200m from the cairn, **Bealach Crosgard** is reached, an obvious pass between east and west (NF 817 298). Head west-south-west from the bealach, initially over steep ground and then, as the gradient decreases, continue around the south side of a small lochan (NF 807 295). Still heading west-south-west, cross hummocky ground until the way ahead is blocked by a deer fence. Follow this fence to the left, downwards, and then across a stile, almost to the shore at NF 801290. Cross the burn immediately ahead and then take a narrow path on the far bank. This leads across a second burn and up the hillside ahead. The path is wet and indistinct, but takes you to the eastern side of Loch nam Faoileann. From here, follow the edge of the loch south and continue down to meet the coastal path, a welcome sight. Finally, this path leads back to an unusual deer-proof bridge, leaving only a short distance to the parking area at Taobh a Tuath Loch Aineort road end.

Descent to Sniseabhal
Descend first from the summit in a south-westerly direction. After about 100m of steep grass, you become reacquainted with the path of ascent. Now follow the arête back towards the north-west, first on the left side, and then, when feasible, move over to the right. A further 500m of mixed ground and you are once more at the north-west summit. The descent from here is a pleasure, and the views are engrossing, but do bear slightly left to avoid mistakenly descending the north-east ridge. It is wise to establish your bearings at this point. In clear conditions your ultimate goal, which should already be visible in the distance, is the building beside the small wood at NF 769 345. In misty conditions you must head almost due north-west. You soon reach a prominent cairn and, as you descend the rocky section below, you should be able to identify a path forking left from **Bealach Carra Dhòmhnuill Ghuirm**. This path slants downwards across the slope before following a gully back to the foot of the mountain. From the base of the gully, go west across flattish ground and then past the pointed outflow of a lochan to reach a small rise. A further 200m to the north-west you intercept a peat track (NF 775 341), only a short distance from the road near Sniseabhal.

BEINN MHÒR

Beinn Mhòr, with a height of 2034ft (620m), is the only hill in the Uists to exceed the 2000ft threshold. However, it also excels in a number of other ways. A fine corrie and impressive summit arête are visually striking and provide spectacular evidence of the erosive power of

*Beinn Mhòr from the
Loch Sgioport road*

glaciers in the Ice Age. It is also the only hill in the area
to boast substantial land cliffs for rock climbing, and the
height and rugged grandeur of this environment create an
ideal habitat for the golden eagle. On rare occasions the
unique local topography near the summit combines with
atmospheric conditions to stage an unexpected delight: a
Brocken Spectre. The sun shining down on the fortunate
visitor may cast an eerie, irridescent shadow on the back-
cloth of mist enveloping the northern corrie.

The ascent of Beinn Mhòr should not be underes-
timated. As with most of the upland walks in the area,
paths are scant and unreliable. Also, the combination
of rough ground and the length of ascent, almost from
sea level, requires a calorific output the equal of many
Munros. In thick fog or strong south-westerly winds, special care must be taken near the summit, as the ground
falls away abruptly on the northern side of the mountain.

Beinn Mhòr may be climbed by a number of different routes, but the two described here, from the Taobh
a Tuath Loch Aineort road end (NF 788 283) and from
Sniseabhal (NF 768 346), cover the main sites of interest
for wildlife and topography. If you can arrange the necessary transport, the two routes may be combined to complete a traverse of the mountain.

WALK 3.5

Beinn Mhòr from Sniseabhal

Start/Finish	Beside main road at NF 768 346 near Sniseabhal, or at track end (NF 775 341)
Distance	From main road (return) 11km; traverse 10km
Total Ascent	650m
Time	4–5hrs
Terrain	Hill and moor
Maps	OS Explorer 453; OS Landanger 22

This is perhaps the most popular route up Beinn Mhòr. It starts close to the main road, the A865, near Sniseabhal, and follows the north-west ridge of the mountain. The gradient is comfortable throughout the climb and, after an initial short, marshy section near the base of the ridge the ground is mainly firm and dry. As you ascend, the ridge gradually narrows, and, with fine views constantly appearing, interest is maintained right to the top.

You may start the walk from the main road itself, but with a reasonably hardy vehicle it is possible to drive up a peat track, and thus reduce the length of the approach march. However, parking space is limited. There is a small parking place on the left after about 500m, and also at the end of the track; but this is restricted, to allow other vehicles to turn.

The route of ascent from Sniseabhal may be combined with the descent to Taobh a Tuath Loch Aineort, to complete a traverse of Beinn Mhòr.

From the main road just south of the bridge, follow the track, threading a way past assorted buildings and poly-tunnels. Pass through a gate and then across the moor to reach a turning area about 1km from the main road. A path, slightly raised above the moorland, continues from the end of the track. Follow this for about 200m to a small coni-cal rise. About 100m to your left there is another rise with a more rounded profile. Go over this, and then continue east, past the left side of a small lochan. Ahead you will see the broad right flank of the ridge dissected by a long, heather-filled gully. The route takes the left side of this gully, and ascends gradually, past a pile of large boulders. As

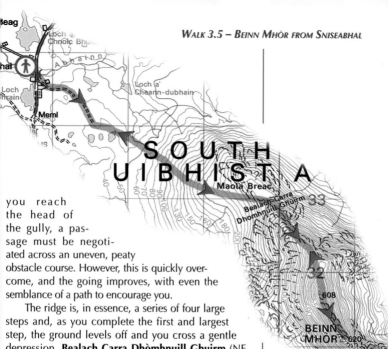

you reach
the head of
the gully, a pas-
sage must be negoti-
ated across an uneven, peaty
obstacle course. However, this is quickly over-
come, and the going improves, with even the
semblance of a path to encourage you.

The ridge is, in essence, a series of four large
steps and, as you complete the first and largest
step, the ground levels off and you cross a gentle
depression, **Bealach Carra Dhòmhnuill Ghuirm** (NF
799 329). The next step is slightly steeper, but arguably
made easier by an abundance of rock outcrops, a natural stone staircase. Another flatter section follows with a
well-constructed cairn standing proudly above its bare,
windswept surroundings; in misty conditions, this serves
as a welcome reminder of the correct route.

At this point, before continuing the climb, it is worth
taking stock, and turning to survey the ground already
covered, the wildness of the moorland giving way to
the green machair of the coastal plain. The next step is
relatively short, and as the ridge begins to narrow, an
easier line is obtained by making a rising traverse up the
right (south-west) side. Having accomplished this, you
once more find yourself on a broad bealach, this time
near the junction with the north-east ridge. Now, pick
your way between the rock outcrops and up to the **north-
west summit** (608m), with its small circle of stones.

121

Beinn Mhòr's northern precipice

A well-defined arête separates the north-west summit from the main summit of **Beinn Mhòr**, but, fortunately, with only a small height increase. Follow the route description given in Walk 3.4 to reach the trig point.

On the way down from the summit, first descend in a south-westerly direction. After about 100m of steep grass, you rejoin the path of ascent. Now follow the directions given in Walk 3.4 for the descent back to Sniseabhal.

WALK 3.6

Beinn Mhòr from Taobh a Tuath Loch Aineort

Start/Finish	Parking space at Taobh a Tuath Loch Aineort road end (NF 788 283)
Distance	10km
Total Ascent	650m
Time	4–5hrs
Terrain	Hill and moor
Maps	OS Explorer 453; OS Landranger 22
Access	Turn east off the A865 at the Ormacleit crossroads (NF 757 305). After approximately 1.2km, turn left at the junction and continue to the road end.

This is the most direct route up Beinn Mhòr and ascends the steep south-western slopes of the mountain. The way down is via the broad south-east ridge to Bealach Crosgard (NF 817 298) and then south-west down to the coast of Loch Aineort. The route provides a rewarding combination of mountain and moorland, ridge walking and bog trotting.

From the parking area, take the obvious path leading eastwards through mixed woodland, a pleasant intro-duction, but there is no time to linger at the start of the walk. The path continues, rising above the shoreline and across the lower hillside, past a small picnic site with natural rock tables. Continue, passing ruins on your right, and then cross a small bridge and an unusual deer-proof stile. Immediately after the bridge, bear left through deep bracken then make a rising traverse across the slopes above the deer fence. After 500m pass through an old gate and then go right to reach the western extremity of **Loch nam Faoileann** (NF 795 289). A short distance further on, a rick-ety stile crosses another fence. Pass over this and continue left along the fence line to the corner. Now leave the fence and, walking north-east for a short distance, you encounter the final man-made obstacle, a deep, dark drainage ditch. A small, wooden bridge provides a convenient crossing.

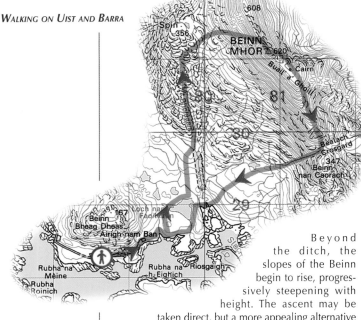

Beyond the ditch, the slopes of the Beinn begin to rise, progressively steepening with height. The ascent may be taken direct, but a more appealing alternative follows the obvious burn, **Allt Bholagair**, which trends diagonally up the hillside towards the minor summit of **Spin**. The gully is narrow and has, in its confines, a series of small waterfalls and assorted foliage to delight the eye.

The summit ridge of Beinn Mhòr, and beyond to the Atlantic

At about two-thirds height a tributary forks off to the right and this takes you to the foot of the final incline. Now aim for the large rocky outcrop at the right-hand end of the ridge above. This ascent may be made mainly on grass, but it is difficult to avoid the scree completely. Be careful! Some of these rocks are distinctly unstable.

The slopes eventually lead to the summit ridge, but it may be necessary to traverse this ridge for a short distance until you find the true top, a trig point surrounded by a stone shelter (NF 809 311). The view is dramatic, particularly to the north-west along the arête, and then down to the coastal machair and the distant Atlantic.

For the onward route from Beinn Mhòr to your starting point at Taobh a Tuath Loch Aineort, follow the directions given in Walk 3.4.

WALK 3.7
Taobh a Tuath Loch Aineort

Start/Finish	Parking area at Taobh a Tuath Loch Aineort road end (NF 788 283)
Distance	4km
Total Ascent	100m
Time	1–2hrs
Terrain	Hill and moor
Maps	OS Explorer 453; OS Landranger 22
Access	Turn east off the A865 at the Ormacleit crossroads (NF 757 305). After approximately 1.2km, turn left at the junction and continue to the road end.

This is a pleasant, scenic walk around the shores of Loch Aineort with paths all the way. Indeed, a number of new paths have recently been developed and these allow access, not only to the coastline, but also to the slopes of Beinn Bheag Dheas. There are many options available and you may pick and mix according to your preferences. This area is frequented by birdwatchers hoping to observe the white-tailed eagle and other species.

The natural picnic site beside the Loch Aineort path

This area of woodland was planted by a local crofter. The combination of shelter and a sunny south-facing aspect has encouraged a proliferation of plant species.

From the parking area, follow the obvious path leading into the woodland, an unusual habitat in the Uists. The way lies through dense foliage between hedges of fuchsia and olearia. ◄

The path continues above the shore, past an unusual picnic site with gneiss tables, a place often used by ornithologists to set up their telescopes. Further on, you begin to see paths forking in different directions, down to the coast and up to the hillside, but on the outward journey it is easier to follow the main, central option. Pass old ruins on your right and soon reach a

small bridge with an interesting stile, specially designed to deter over-enthusiastic stag parties!

Beyond the bridge the path continues, following the coast around the next headland. The going remains dry until you turn north into the next inlet (NF 800 287). Here the path deteriorates, signalling the time to turn back.

Once past the bridge on the return walk, it is worth making minor detours from the main track. The various paths ascending the hillside soon provide enough height to give excellent views across Loch Aineort, and those by the shore pass through woodland beside small tranquil bays. Whichever route you take, it is almost impossible to get lost. Sooner or later you will undoubtedly return to the main path that leads you back to your starting point.

The area around **Loch Aineort** has a turbulent history. There is a place at the head of the Loch called Rubh' an Tigh-mhàil ('The Rent House Point'), named after a macabre encounter in the time of Clanranald. It is said that a man with the sinister title Gille Padra Dubh ('dark servant of Patrick') came to visit the factor to pay his rent: a sackful of grain. The factor foolishly questioned the quantity of grain. Gille Padra Dubh grabbed the factor, cut his throat and let the blood flow into the sack. 'It'll be full now,' he said.

WALK 3.8
Stulaigh

Start/Finish	The bend on the Lasgair road (NF 786 202)
Distance	13km
Total Ascent	800m
Time	5–6hrs
Terrain	Hill and moor
Maps	OS Explorer 453; OS Landranger 22, 31
Access	Turn off the Lochboisdale road to Lasgair (NF 785 201).

A walk of continuous interest which heads out to the long-abandoned settlement at Caolas Stulaigh, and then returns via the hills overlooking Lochboisdale. The walk is reasonably strenuous, much of it over pathless hill country, but it is possible to shorten the route if necessary. Waterproof boots are advisable, mainly to wade through the wet introductory section. If conditions are very wet, a drier, if slightly longer, alternative start is available by taking the track off the main road about 50m west of the bend at NF 783 204. After crossing the bridge, turn sharp right close to the water before heading south-east to join the normal route.

A clear day is recommended for tackling this route, as navigation is tricky in misty conditions.

Leave the bend on the Lasgair road, and walk past a house on the corner to reach the lane heading down to the shore. The ground looks innocent enough, but tread gingerly between the drier clumps of rushes. There are one or two very wet sections, even in the height of a Hebridean summer. After negotiating the damp introduction, cross the double-gated bridge to reach the start of the clearly defined track marked on the OS map. There are false leads veering prematurely north. Ignore these, and after 1km of pleasant walking, you should encounter the old **water pumping station** (NF 797 208). Fork left just before this building, following a faint trail across a flat, bouncy carpet of blanket bog.

Looking to the north-east there is a clear gap, **Bealach na Diollaid** (Explorer map) between the main hill of Triuirebheinn and its lesser neighbour Cleit. Leave the path and take a gradually rising traverse across the heather-covered hillside to reach this gap. A grand view awaits you. Moving over the rise towards the north-east, **Loch nan Arm** (Explorer map) comes into view, nestling in its corrie. Further distant is Bealach a' Chaolais, the passage to your outward destination. The loch may be passed on either side, but the northern option is preferable: a friendly mixture of moss and deep heather cushioning the descent towards the water. After the loch, a gentle climb past an old ruin brings you to a path, now only vague, but no doubt well trodden in the past.

Crossing the watershed, the path descends through a tall gate and then down a narrow valley to the coast beside **Caolas Stulaigh**. A number of ruined dwellings remain, sitting on a small flat shelf of land above the shore. This must have been an amazing place to live, the land all around rising steep and inhospitable. It is worth conducting a brief exploration of the area. Just to the south-east, a short distance offshore, lies the island of Stulaigh, once renowned for its ornamental building stone. Otters may be visible, close offshore.

Although it is tempting to continue to follow the coast south, the route up **Triuirebhein** is blocked by a deer fence. It is wiser to commence the return journey by retracing your steps back through the gate. Any disappointment in going over the same ground is quickly dispelled. The valley below the gate is a garden of wild flowers in the springtime. After passing through the gate and back over the watershed, you once again reach the old ruin observed on the outward walk. Now, instead of descending to the loch, take the track slanting left up the hillside and round into a narrow valley leading to

129

Looking over Loch nan Arm to Loch Stulabhal

Along the way it is worth taking time to scan the skies overhead for golden eagles and other raptors.

the col (NF 814 224). There are great views south-east to the coast, and also north-west over Loch nan Arm to Loch Stulabhal.

The ascent of Triuirebheinn starts south-west from the col up steep mixed ground, and a course must be navigated around a series of rocky outcrops. However, height is soon gained, and the climb leads up to the broad northern shoulder of the hill. The way to the summit from here appears formidable, but, fortunately, the scale is deceptive. The top, decorated with a minimalist cairn, is reached much more quickly than anticipated. ◄

The descent from Triuirebheinn south to **Bealach an Easain** is steep and rocky in places, and care is needed, as there are significant cliffs, often hidden from above. From the Bealach, it is worth making a slight detour to a cave, **Uamh Àrd** (Explorer map), believed, like many others, to have provided refuge for Bonnie Prince Charlie. About 250m south-east of the Bealach is a small cliff with an impressive overhang (NF 813 202). Pass under this overhang and then climb up the steep hillside further to

the east. You will notice a recess in the rock face higher up – the cave entrance. The easiest access is along an airy ledge traversing in from the right.

Uamh Àrd – refuge of Bonnie Prince Charlie?

    Descend back to the Bealach before the final haul to **Beinn Ruigh Choinnich**. There are one or two false summits to taunt you on the ascent, but finally you reach a substantial cairn, the real top. Moving a few metres to the west, you reap the reward for this endeavour, an extensive panorama over Loch Baghasdail and beyond.

BEN KENNETH HILL RACE

Beinn Ruigh Choinnich or Ben Kenneth, as it is sometimes known, is the venue for a hill race, starting in Lochboisdale, and held annually at the beginning of August. Some competitors take the drier route around the bay near the start, but other athletes prefer to swim across the inlet to the foot of the hill.

    This annual hill race has a historical precedent. In the days of the Clearances, in the mid-19th century, many of the people removed from their land were taken to Lochboisdale to be transported overseas. Three brothers from Benbecula were about to board ship, when the youngest, a teenage lad, broke free and escaped to the moors. Howling dogs pursued him, but he daringly evaded capture by scaling the steep, rocky slopes of Beinn Ruigh Choinnich. After surviving for weeks in the hills, he returned home to recount the tale.

The final section of the route drops down the northwestern slopes of Beinn Ruigh Choinnich, aiming to rejoin the outward path at NF 792 207. The descent is steep at first, but the gradient soon relents and a series of sheep tracks help guide you back to your destination. After reaching the path, a short walk takes you back to the bridge near the start.

WALK 3.9

Gleann Dail bho Dheas

Start/Finish	Park close to the end of the road at Gleann Dail bho Dheas (NF 791 154), but avoid the turning place used by local buses
Distance	12km
Total Ascent	400m
Time	5–6hrs
Terrain	Hill and moor
Maps	OS Explorer 453; OS Landranger 31

The area in the extreme south-east of South Uist is rarely visited today, except by those employed in fish farming operations. However, in the past, particularly in the 19th century, there was extensive settlement, accessed by well-constructed tracks and bridleways. This walk uses these tracks in combination with open moorland to produce a fine circuit. However, the route is relatively long and arduous and is best tackled in spring or summer when the surface is more user-friendly. In winter, even parts of the track turn into a quagmire.

The route described here starts at Gleann Dail bho Dheas and goes in an anti-clockwise direction to take advantage of a long downhill section of moorland.

Follow the track north from the end of the road, passing through two gates. As you reach the top of the rise ahead, the view opens up north towards Lochboisdale and Beinn Mhòr. Abandon the track at the highest point and climb east up the heathery slopes of **Marabhal**. The terrain is firm and dry and the summit cairn is easily attained, revealing an extensive southern panorama over Eriskay and Barra. However, our route heads east, making a gradual descent to the small lochan at NF 807 158. From here, the target is the head of **Loch Marulaigh** (NF 821 159). This stretch may be wet, and you might need to deviate from the direct line to avoid the boggiest sections. On the other hand, there should be ample opportunity to observe plants favouring this marshy habitat. For the last kilometre, the route follows the southern shore of the loch, where the sheltered waters

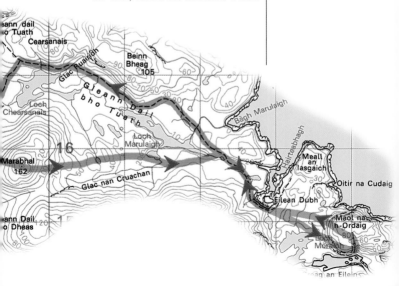

The track north from Glean Dail bho Dheas

You pass a number of ruined black houses along the track, their thick walls and rounded corners well adapted for surviving the rigours of this testing environment.

have created a suitable location for mooring fish farming cages.

After crossing the burn at the end of Loch Marulaigh, a short walk north-east brings you to the track from Gleann Dail bho Tuath. The way is now clear: south-east to the bay opposite **Eilean Dubh**, 'the black island' (NF 829 153). ◄

The track curves round the southern end of the bay where a well-preserved sea wall protects the vulnerable shoreline. The main path ends on the east side of the bay, but faint tracks do continue further south-east, first to **Loch Mòraibh** and then on towards **Maol na h-Ordaig**. If you venture this far – the eastern extremity of South Uist – there is a fine view north along the mountainous eastern seaboard of the island. The slopes of Beinn Mhòr and Thacla may be seen, falling steeply to the Little Minch.

Returning to the main track near Eilean Dubh, the route back to the start should be relatively straightforward. The track through **Gleann Dail bho Tuath** is well defined and easy to follow. Only the occasional diversion is required – for example crossing the burn at NF 819 163, where the old bridge has collapsed. However, some of the ground may be very wet. Be alert at the western end of **Loch Chearsanais** for the path forking south to **Gleann Dail bho Dheas**. Once you have turned left at this junction, the final stretch to the finish should provide comfortable walking.

WALK 3.10
Eriskay (Eirisgeigh)

Start/Finish	Eriskay shop (NF 787 118) (ask in the shop for the best place to park)
Distance	7km
Total Ascent	250m
Time	3–4hrs
Terrain	Hill and sandy coast
Maps	OS Explorer 453; OS Landranger 31

Eriskay is only a small island, 5km long and 3km wide, yet it contains remarkable scenic variety, and also historic sites. The beach on the west side of the island, Coilleag a' Phrionnsa, is said to be the place where Bonnie Prince Charlie first landed on Scottish soil after returning from France in 1745. More recently, during the Second World War, the SS *Politician* was wrecked on a reef in the Sound of Eriskay (Caolas Eirisgeigh). Part of the ship's cargo, cases of Scotch whisky, was rescued and hidden by the enterprising islanders. The happenings surrounding this legendary event formed the basis of Compton Mackenzie's book and the subsequent classic film *Whisky Galore*. Even today, when house foundations are being excavated, samples of this famous booty are occasionally unearthed.

Until recently, transport to Eriskay from South Uist was by a small ferry, which was tide dependent. However, the completion of the causeway in 2001 meant that access was now possible at any time. Eriskay forms part of the link between South Uist and Barra. The car ferry to Barra leaves from a pier on the west coast of the Island.

The walk outlined below visits Eriskay's more remote eastern shore before returning west over Beinn Sciathan to drop down to the beautiful bay, Coilleag a' Phrionnsa.

Rubh' an
t-Seana Bhalla
Rubha
Bàn
Jetty
Ph
cho
Haunn
Bun a'Mhuillinn
Cemys
Rubha Chlaidh
Am
Baile
Cairns
△185
Beinn Sciathan
Sloc a
Loch
Dubh
Rònais
Coilleag a'
Phrionnsa
Mèml
Coilleag
Loch
Cracabhaig
Beinn
Cracabhaig
71
●102
Na
Pàirceanan

Follow the road uphill from the shop until you reach a sharp bend to the right. Now leave the road and aim for a small scree slope on the northern side of **Beinn Sciathan.** You soon pass a ruined house with a rusty roof, and then a gradual ascent leads to a gate allowing access to the open hillside. Vague paths wander across the slopes and under the apron of scree to reach the north-eastern spur of the Beinn. You can head directly up the spur to the summit, but, if time permits, a brief exploration of the eastern side of the island is a rewarding addition. On a clear day there are fine views to the Inner Hebrides, from Skye round to Rùm and then the more distant isles of Mull, Coll and Tiree.

The Cuillin Hills of Skye

If you venture east of the spur, you first pass above **Loch Dubhat**, and then, moving south, the ground falls abruptly to the impressive, steep-sided inlet between **Rònais** and **Rubha Basadearn** (NF 804 111). However, caution is required as the slopes are steep and the drop considerable. On the more gentle ground further south the walking is excellent – grass interspersed with rocky outcrops. The grass is conveniently short, expertly manicured by a rare native of the island, the Eriskay Pony. ▶

After following the coast for a short distance, head inland up to the trig point on Beinn Sciathan. This is a good place to pause, as in addition to the views east you may now survey the panorama south-east to Barra. To the north-west, the causeway may be seen curving round to the shores of South Uist.

Descend from the summit in a south-westerly direction, but move carefully, for the ground is steep and rocky. A gate breaches the fence about 400m west of **Loch Cracabhaig**. Once through the gate, you may encounter way markers, but these lead directly to the village. For a longer walk, cut across open land to the west of the loch and head for the **building** at NF 792 107. A gravel track leads down from this building to the road. On reaching the road, go north-west through the small hamlet of **Coilleag** and then fork left at the junction where a side road descends towards the Barra ferry terminal. About 50m from the junction, a path leads right, past a house and then down towards the shore, **Coilleag a' Phrionnsa**. Follow the track above the beach north, to a cairn marking the place where Bonnie Prince Charlie came ashore. In this area, in the summer, you might spot a pink flower, the Prince's flower, the seeds of which were apparently dropped by the Prince as he made landfall.

The remainder of the route is relatively relaxing, just follow the beach to its northern end. It is worth scanning the strand line as you go. At certain times of the year you may find a cornucopia of seashells, particularly from razor fish inhabiting the shallow waters offshore. At the end of the beach, a path leads up past a picnic site to join the road once again. Bear left, following the road towards

The Eriskay Pony is the last surviving native pony from the Outer Hebrides. Although numbers declined to only 20 in the early 1970s, they have since rallied, rising to almost 500 ponies worldwide.

Coilleag a' Phrionnsa

the village. After passing the café (Am Politician), take a right turn back to the shop. If you haven't yet met the native ponies, this is where you may find them; they seem attracted to the bright lights of Eriskay village!

MACHAIR WAY

The Machair Way is a long walk of almost 40km along the western coastline of South Uist. The walk runs from Pol a' Charra in the south (NF 747 143) to Cill Amhlaidh in the north (NF 752 459). The route follows a series of paths and tracks along the dunes and across the internationally acclaimed machair environment. It is perhaps best seen in early summer when the wild flowers are at their peak. However, at that time of year, it is important not to stray over cultivated land, or disturb ground-nesting birds.

The complete walk is not covered in this guide, but the route is relatively easy to follow, with tracks for most of the Way clearly marked on the OS maps (Landranger 22 and 31). However, many of the original way markers have now disappeared. Occasionally, fences block the obvious route, forcing you to divert to the beach, but this is a pleasant alternative. The only potentially problematic section involves crossing the MOD danger area north of Loch Groigearraidh (NF 759 398). If the range is active, red flags will provide a warning, and, if necessary, military personnel will be available to provide onward transport. Details of range activities are posted in local shops. If in doubt, contact the Range Controller on 01870 604449.

The two walks described below cover relatively short sections of the Way, but both provide a worthwhile flavour of the longer walk. They also pass sites of historical importance.

WALK 3.11
Tobha Mòr

Start/Finish	Car park beside Howmore Church (NF 757 364)
Distance	5km
Total Ascent	Minimal
Time	1–2hrs
Terrain	Machair and sandy coast
Maps	OS Explorer 453; OS Landranger 22

This is a relatively short, low-level walk, but it gives a good taste of the landscape encountered on the much longer Machair Way. The route follows a figure-of-eight course, which samples both the machair and neighbouring sections of coastline. The walk starts close to the Tobha Mòr chapels and graveyard, important historical sites, possibly dating back as far as the 13th century. Background on these sites is provided by an information display beside the church car park.

Go west from the car park, past the **church** and through a gate. At the junction with the main track, turn left and continue through another gate and over the bridge. As the

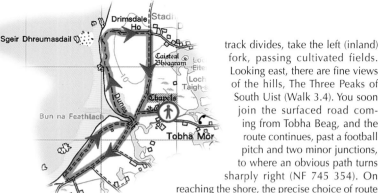

track divides, take the left (inland) fork, passing cultivated fields. Looking east, there are fine views of the hills, The Three Peaks of South Uist (Walk 3.4). You soon join the surfaced road coming from Tobha Beag, and the route continues, past a football pitch and two minor junctions, to where an obvious path turns sharply right (NF 745 354). On reaching the shore, the precise choice of route north depends upon your preference. The beach is a good option, especially at low tide, but the dunes and machair are also attractive, particularly with the floral adornment of spring and early summer. There is plenty of bird life to focus your attention, and you may even spot the great yellow bumblebee. As you approach the river mouth at **Bun na Feathlach**, you may be tempted to wade across. This is not recommended. It is wiser, safer and much drier to head back to the bridge.

The historic site at Tobha Mòr

North of the bridge, take the route beside the shore. Initially, you have a choice: the beach, the dune crest, or the track along the edge of the machair. However, further north, a fence forces all routes down to the coast. Continue, passing outcrops of banded gneiss, to where a rocky promontory, **Sgeir Dhreumasdail**, signals time for the return inland. Pass through the gate and then along strips of unploughed machair to the crossroads at NF 757 375 beside **Drimsdale House**. Bear right, following the track back to Howmore Church. To the left, on an island in the middle of **Loch an Eilein**, is a ruined castle, Caisteal Bheagram, believed to date from the same period as the chapel at Tobha Mòr.

WALK 3.12
Aisgernis/Cladh Hàlainn

Start/Finish	Park near the clubhouse at Askernish Golf Course (NF 730 240)
Distance	5km
Total Ascent	100m
Time	2hrs
Terrain	Machair and sandy coast
Maps	OS Explorer 453; OS Landranger 22, 31

This is shortish walk along the coastline and across the machair between Aisgernis and Cladh Hàlainn, close to the recently rediscovered Askernish Golf Course. The course was designed by legendary golfer Old Tom Morris back in the late 19th century, only to disappear for most of the 20th century. It is a fine links course in a superb situation and is currently being restored to its former glory.

The walk may be done in either direction, starting at Aisgernis or Cladh Hàlainn. In the interests of safety, while walking close to the golf course, it is wise to scan the nearby tees and fairways to check for golfers about to play their shots, and be ready to take evasive action if necessary.

From the **clubhouse**, follow tracks west across the golf course and up to the sand dunes. You are greeted by a splendid view south along the shore and on towards Barra. This view is your focus and inspiration over the next 2km. Tread warily past the seventh tee and continue along the dune ridge. The golf holes follow you along the coast, but it would require a severe sliced shot to interrupt your progress! If you feel vulnerable, drop down to the beach instead. It is a rewarding walk along beach or dune, with a variety of sea birds close by.

Prehistoric roundhouses at Cladh Hàlainn

A break in the dunes at NF 728 221, just before a prominent picnic site, marks the point of your departure inland. Follow an obvious track, and after 400m you reach **Cladh Hàlainn**, a highly significant Bronze Age site, where mummified remains were recently discovered. Most of the excavations have now been in-filled, but display boards provide detailed information.

Continue south-east around the **cemetery**, heading towards the transmission mast. The route now turns north, following the track past the east side of the cemetery and then through a gate. The general way ahead is now clear, towards the clubhouse, which is just visible in the far distance. However, there are various options, as many tracks criss-cross the machair.

The most direct route runs close to the reed beds beside **Loch Hallan**, and then between cultivated fields, favoured, in season, by flocks of geese. In the distance are the South Uist hills and the long ridge of Beinn Mhòr.

If you prefer to gloat over the struggles and frustrations of the golfing fraternity, then follow tracks further west around the eastern edge of the course. This option is probably more scenic, and at dusk you will surely be entertained by rabbits, able to scuttle happily in the dimming light, no longer in fear of the daylight bombardment from golf balls.

Presently, you will need to veer back inland, choosing one of the tracks leading back to the clubhouse, where, in the summer months, there is the welcome attraction of a range of refreshments. ▶

While in this area, it is worth visiting Kildonan Museum (NF 747 275), and also Flora MacDonald's birthplace (NF 741 269), both easily accessed from the main road.

4 BARRA
Barraigh

Barra's Atlantic coastline

INTRODUCTION

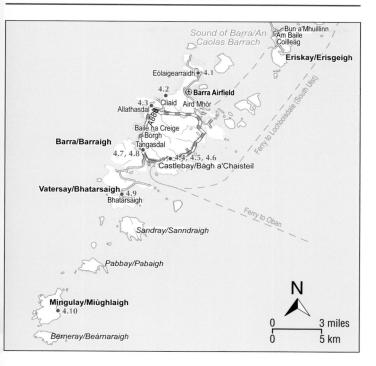

Barra is a picturesque island, often regarded as one of the most beautiful in the UK. In many ways it encapsulates, in miniature, the attractions of the Outer Hebrides as a whole: white sand beaches and clear, blue water set against a backdrop of hill and sky.

Barra's compactness enables the walker to sample a wide variety of scenery in the same day. Indeed, a number of walks, such as Cliaid and Beinn Tangabhal (Walks 4.2, 4.8), combine both hill and beach.

Barra's circular road, the A888, gives relatively easy access to almost all parts of the island. Castlebay is Barra's main population and service centre, and it also provides the ferry link to Oban and Lochboisdale.

WALK 4.1
Barra's northern peninsula

Start/Finish	Car park near the cemetery at Cille Bharra (NF 706 073)
Distance	8km; 5km for shorter option
Total Ascent	150m
Time	4–5hrs
Terrain	Hill and sandy coast
Maps	OS Explorer 452; OS Landranger 31

This is an exhilarating walk, providing majestic views over northern Barra. Most of the terrain is straightforward, over grassy hills and along beaches, and there is also some road walking. Although most of the ground is dry, there may be short damp sections, and appropriate footwear should be worn. It is well worth carrying binoculars for watching wildlife.

Navigation on the route should not be a problem: there are a number of marker posts to guide you over the hills and across the machair.

The walk starts from the car park beside the cemetery at Cille Bharra, a notable historic site. Enclosed within the perimeter wall are the ruins of church buildings possibly dating from the 12th century. Compton Mackenzie, the author of *Whisky Galore*, is buried in the upper part of the graveyard.

Walk north-west along the road until you reach the sharp bend beneath **Dùn Sgùrabhal** (NF 697 083). Along this stretch, in the early summer, you may well hear the distinctive, rasping call of the corncrake.

On reaching the bend, go through the gate to access the hillside on your left. The climb up the dun is fairly steep, but relatively short, and, as you gain height, fine views appear to the north, over the shingle beach to Beinn Sgùrabhal and on towards Fiaraigh and the Uists. At the top, it is easy to see why this site was chosen. This dun, like other Iron Age forts in Barra, occupies an imposing, almost impregnable position, relatively easy to defend against marauding invaders.

From the dun, continue south-east to **Beinn Eòlaigearraidh**, picking up a faint trail beside the way markers. It is worth taking this walk at a leisurely pace, allowing you to absorb the surrounding grandeur. To your right, beside the Atlantic, the western beaches are gradually revealed, and in the springtime, the soft grass underfoot is embroidered with a sea of pale yellow primroses. As you summit the Beinn, the true

Dùn Sgùrabhal perched above the Atlantic

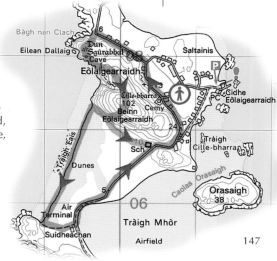

extent of Barra's beach landscape becomes apparent: to the west, the white sands of Tràigh Eais, and to the east, Tràigh Mhòr, Barra's improbable airfield.

Descend in a westerly direction down the grassy slopes towards the northern end of **Tràigh Eais**. Again, take your time. This is one of the prime places on Barra for spotting the Adder's tongue fern and, in the summer months, there are literally hundreds of plant species to be seen in the area, including a variety of orchids. At the foot of the hill, a gate gives access to the beach.

At this point there are different options. If you prefer a shorter walk, you may return from the beach, through the gate, and then follow the track south-west to join the road near **Eòlaigearraidh School** (NF 703 068). The road then leads you back to the car park. To continue on the longer walk, head south down the wonderful expanse of Tràigh Eais. As you stroll along, you will undoubtedly be accompanied, at close quarters, by oystercatchers and a variety of gulls. In addition, if you closely scan the western horizon, you may see gannets diving in offshore waters.

All too soon, you reach the southern end of the beach and, as you turn inland, you once more encounter the marker posts, leading across the machair and over a

Tràigh Mhòr – Barra's airfield

stile to the road. **Suidheachan**, the large building on your right, was once the home of author Compton MacKenzie. The route back to the start from here follows the road north, but, if time permits, the airport café provides a welcome refreshment stop. ▶

If your schedule coincides with a flight, you will have a grandstand view of the world's only regular tidal airport.

WALK 4.2
Cliaid

Start/Finish	Beside the Cliaid road near the western end of the beach (NF 668 049)
Distance	4.5km
Total Ascent	220m
Time	3hrs
Terrain	Hill and sandy coast
Maps	OS Explorer 452; OS Landranger 31

This walk combines varied coastal scenery with a short hill walk up Beinn Chliaid, which provides superb views over the northern part of the island. The walk may be completed comfortably in a morning or afternoon. It is best done at low tide to allow easier access to the arch and caves. The route involves a small amount of scrambling. Care must be taken when moving over coastal rocks; the surfaces are often wet and slippery. At high tide the caves may become inaccessible.

Head east from the starting point and descend onto the broad expanse of beach. A pleasant walk along the sand brings you to a small rocky promontory. The next section is tide dependent. At very low tide, the rocks may be bypassed to access a narrow inlet backed by a cave (NF 673 049). After exploring the cave, you will notice a slender arch veering east-wards, dissecting the cliff face. This is the most interesting option. Once through

the arch, a scramble up the rocks on the left leads you round to reach the grassy slopes above.

If the tide is further in, a short scramble over the promontory is necessary to access the cave and arch. However, take care! If the arch is flooded, you will need to turn back before scrambling up rocks to the grass above. At high tide, it is wise to bypass the cave altogether and head straight for the grassy slopes above the end of the beach.

About 20m above the shore, a path continues towards the east, rising gently beneath a series of small, dark cliffs. There is severe erosion in places, and at one point the path goes perilously close to the edge. However, it soon accesses a broad, grassy terrace. On the left you pass a number of large boulders, one with a strange indentation resembling a sinister footprint. From here, you may continue to explore the coastline with its numerous caves and geos, but be aware that the rocks are often slippery and insecure. Our route follows the terrace, gradually ascending diagonally up the hillside.

After approximately 400m, an interesting archaeological site is passed on the left (NF 677 048), although its origins are uncertain. Now, as the gradient decreases, bear right, up the hillside towards **Beinn Chliaid**. The ground is steep at first, but the angle soon relents as you scale the broad shoulder to the north of the summit. Great views become apparent: west along Cliaid beach towards Ceann Àird Ghrèin, and north-east to the amazing tombolo of northern Barra with Tràigh Eais and Tràigh Mhòr, home to the island's airport. Continue south over the shoulder and up a final rise to the summit, marked by a tiny cairn.

On the way down, it is easy to become entrapped by a network of barbed wire fences. To avoid these fences, first return north for 200m to the top of a gully dropping down to the west. Descend this gully past an old wall and then trend right, following the course of a burn downwards towards the beach. About 100m above the beach, take a path leading off to the right. The path narrows below some cliffs, but takes you round the end of the fence. After crossing a small gully, it is possible to scramble down the rocks and back to the beach for the return to your starting point.

WALK 4.3

Allathasdal

Start/Finish	Parking area close to the cemetery near Cuidhir (NF 662 036)
Distance	8km
Total Ascent	200m
Time	2–3hrs
Terrain	Moor and sandy coast
Maps	OS Explorer 452; OS Landranger 31

A varied walk, which combines pasture and moorland with fine coastal scenery. The route also visits archaeological sites. For the most part, the ground provides dry, comfortable walking, and a series of marker posts were set up by the Ranger service to help guide you up the valley. However, although the posts avoid the boggiest areas, it is still advisable to wear sturdy, waterproof footwear.

A gate gives access to the field across from the **cemetery**. In the south-eastern corner of this field, marker posts lead up through a gully. Follow these posts to the obvious hilltop fortification, **Dùn Chuidhir**. Although the dun dates from the Iron Age, this site, with its commanding defensive location, is believed to have been occupied more recently by Redcoats in 1746.

Heading south-east from the dun, markers guide you across grazing land and then over the burn which drains the **Allathasdal valley**. As you proceed up the valley, you pass a number of ruined black houses, evidence of a community once densely populated, but later decimated by the Clearances of the mid-19th century.

Entering the upper valley, the pasture gives way to moorland, and buzzards may commonly be seen scanning the hillside for prey. In this area (NF 671 024), the marker posts suddenly diverge, one route leading to the Aisled House, **Taigh Talamhanta**, and the other veering more steeply up the valley side towards **Dùn Bharpa**. If you wish to visit both sites, it is best to head first to Taigh Talamhanta. This site was excavated in the 1950s

Tràigh Hamara

to reveal an aisled farmhouse dating from the Iron Age. Although much of the detail is now hidden, the outline remains visible.

The direct route from here to the dun goes up a gradual incline in a west-south-westerly direction for about 800m. However, there are no markers and the ground is wet, soft and boggy. The alternative, drier option, involves returning to the point where the paths diverge and then climbing south to reach Dùn Bharpa. Confusingly named, this dun is in fact a chambered cairn from the Neolithic period, believed to be about 5500 years old.

The way now continues south into the **Borgh valley**. First, cross the stile immediately east of the cairn and then descend the hillside, heading south to the **building** at NF 673 014. ▶

A track now leads west through **Baile na Creige** to reach the junction with the island's circular road. Although the homeward route mainly follows this road, you will not be disappointed. Along the way, you will pass some wonderful west coast scenery.

Leaving the junction, the road closely follows the shore, first beside the estuary; but as you round the bend

This refurbished black house was formerly a museum, but closed as a result of storm damage in 2005.

curving northwards, beneath you appears the exquisite **Tràigh Hamara** (Explorer map), its white sands fringed by clear blue waters of aquamarine, turquoise and sapphire. Further north, near the junction at NF 658 031, a gate provides access to the machair, and, beyond the dunes, to another beautiful beach beside the aptly nicknamed Seal Bay. Grey seals are frequently seen here, basking on the skerries just offshore. Returning to the road, a short walk takes you back to the starting point.

BARRA'S CENTRAL HILLS

The hills stretching north from Sheabhal to Beinn Bheireasaigh, which are enclosed by Barra's circular road, form a sinuous upland spine dividing the east and west sides of the island. The following three walks, The Barra Watershed, Barra's highest hills and Central Barra, explore this region, and also visit Barra's highest summit, Sheabhal. Although the terrain in this area offers excellent, dry walking for the most part, stout footwear is required, as short sections are rough and sometimes boggy. A map and compass are also essential. Despite Barra being a small island, it is surprisingly easy to get lost!

WALK 4.4

The Barra Watershed

Start	Car park west of the high point (102m) on the road between Castlebay and Brèibhig (NL 679 987)
Finish	Western end of Loch an Duin (NF 688 033)
Distance	6km
Total Ascent	600m
Time	3hrs
Terrain	Hill and moor
Maps	OS Explorer 452; OS Landranger 31

The Barra Watershed, following Barra's central spine, runs from south to north, starting at the foot of Sheabhal. The suggested route ends at Loch an Duin, so transport will be needed back to the start. A shorter walk, taking in Sheabhal and its satellites, but returning to the start point, is described in route 4.5.

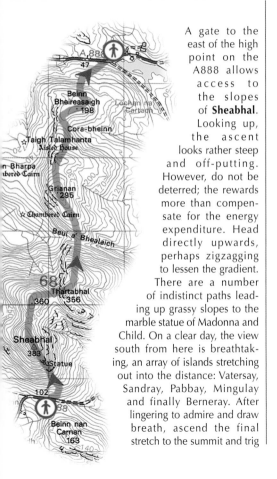

A gate to the east of the high point on the A888 allows access to the slopes of **Sheabhal**. Looking up, the ascent looks rather steep and off-putting. However, do not be deterred; the rewards more than compensate for the energy expenditure. Head directly upwards, perhaps zigzagging to lessen the gradient. There are a number of indistinct paths leading up grassy slopes to the marble statue of Madonna and Child. On a clear day, the view south from here is breathtaking, an array of islands stretching out into the distance: Vatersay, Sandray, Pabbay, Mingulay and finally Berneray. After lingering to admire and draw breath, ascend the final stretch to the summit and trig

The view south from Sheabhal's statue

A race from Castlebay to the summit of Sheabhal and back takes place every summer. The record time of 26 minutes is held by local man, Calum Maclean.

point. The easiest route follows the vague tracks just left of the rocky buttress. ◄

Having reached Sheabhal's summit, the most strenuous part of the walk is completed. Go along the broad ridge, first north-north-west, and then north to the summit and cairn at spot height 360m. Looking over to the Atlantic, you can see the Borgh valley stretching out to the machair and onwards to Gob Bhuirgh. Changing direction, now head east-north-east down to the col at NF 681 001. From there, a short climb brings you to **Thartabhal**.

From Thartabhal's cairn, the route drops to **Beul a' Bhealaich**. It is wise to descend in an east-north-easterly direction to avoid the principal rocky sections. Whatever route is chosen, care is required, as the descent over mixed terrain is steep. The ground flattens out at the Beul, in past days a well-used route between the east and west sides of the island.

As the walk continues, there is another change of direction, this time north-west. The climb up **Grianan**, the next hill, is steep at first, but the gradient soon relents to provide a pleasant ascent up a broad ridge. However, the convex slopes leave you guessing where the summit really is. Indeed, you are still left wondering even when you finally reach the top, to find a cairn of miniscule proportions!

Leaving the summit, the way now lies north over open country with fine views east and west: excellent walking. The final cairn on **Beinn Bheireasaigh** is soon reached. The descent from here is slightly awkward, and dangerous in mist. Head west at first to avoid a short precipitous section, and then, as you continue north-east over mixed ground, be wary of rocky steps. You presently reach the end of the track beside **Loch an Dùin**, and a gate provides access to the road.

WALK 4.5
Barra's highest hills

Start/Finish	Car park west of the high point (102m) on the road between Castlebay and Brèibhig (NL 679 987)
Distance	5km
Total Ascent	400m
Time	2–3hrs
Terrain	Hill
Maps	OS Explorer 452; OS Landranger 31

This route first climbs Sheabhal, and then follows Walk 4.4 as far as the summit of Thartabhal (NF 682 001). The way back to the start makes a descending traverse across Sheabhal's eastern slopes.

Follow the directions for Walk 4.4 until you reach the summit of **Thartabhal** (356m), Barra's second highest named hill.

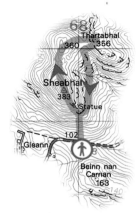

The most appropriate return route will depend on the weather. The first option provides more variety, but is not recommended in wet or misty conditions as the ground may be slippery and there are no reliable paths.

First retrace your steps to the col beside Thartabhal (NF 681 001). From here, the route goes south, dropping slightly at first, and then traversing across Sheabhal's eastern slopes. You encounter a number of small gullies and rocky slabs en route, but obstacles may easily be avoided. If you follow the contours and maintain height, you will presently emerge on Sheabhal's south-east ridge, just below the **statue**. A steep, grassy descent from here takes you back to the road.

If it is misty, it is wiser to return from Thartabhal to the trig point on Sheabhal, and then back down past the statue to the road.

Looking north to the Uists

WALK 4.6
Central Barra

Start/Finish	Car park west of the high point (102m) on the road between Castlebay and Brèibhig (NL 679 987)
Distance	16km
Total Ascent	1000m
Time	6–8hrs
Terrain	Hill
Maps	OS Explorer 452; OS Landranger 31

A long, but very rewarding route, which makes a circuit of Barra's central massif, and includes highlights from three other walks. The route first follows Walk 4.4 (Barra Watershed), before linking with Walk 4.3 (Allathasdal) and the latter half of Walk 4.5 (Barra's highest hills).

Map continued on page 160

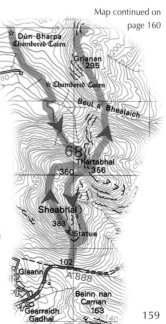

Follow the directions for Walk 4.4 as far as **Loch an Dùin** (NF 688 033).

From the gate beside Loch an Dùin, follow the road west for a distance of 3km until you reach the cemetery near **Dùn Chuidhir** (NF 662 036), the starting point for the Allathasdal walk (Walk 4.3). Follow the directions for this route until you reach **Dùn Bharpa** (NF 672 019). Leaving the dun, cross the stile over the adjacent fence. Now, instead of descending to the old museum, contour round towards the south-east to reach a second **chambered cairn** (NF 677 012).

A steep-sided tributary valley is visible to the south, and is your next destination (NF 677 009). Move in this general direction, diverting east for a short distance to cross the main valley burn. On reaching the tributary, you find an extraordinary

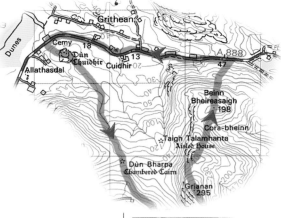

place, certainly worth further exploration. The water issues from a narrow cleft in the hillside. It is possible to enter this dark, murky world, but caution is required. The rock is treacherous – wet and extremely slimy.

Inside the narrow cleft at NF 677 009

Back in the daylight, the route ascends the left flank of the burn, curving upwards across the valley side. It is safer to keep well back from the edge, away from the water. The burn flows through a series of small, deceptively deep ravines.

You steadily gain height and, as you move upwards past the source of the burn, the route merges with the neighbouring valley at NF 681 004. From here, a short, stiff climb brings you back to the col (NF 681 001) visited earlier in the day.

The completion of the route back from the col to the starting point is described in Walk 4.5.

WALK 4.7
Dùn Bàn

Start/Finish	Beside the phone box at Tangasdal, 3km west of Castlebay (NF 649 001)
Distance	5km
Total Ascent	100m
Time	2–3hrs
Terrain	Rocky coast and sandy coast
Maps	OS Explorer 452; OS Landranger 31

This is a fine walk to a historical site in an impressive location, sampling a variety of habitats. Although relatively short, the walk provides a superb introduction to Barra's magnificent west coast with its rocky headlands and pristine beaches.

A stile and gate opposite the phone box give access to the machair. There are a number of way markers to help guide you along the route to Dùn Bàn.

Walk across pasture towards the shore of **Loch Tangasdal**. On an islet towards the eastern end of the loch is the ruin of Macleod's Tower, dating from the 15th century, but believed to be built over the site of a much older

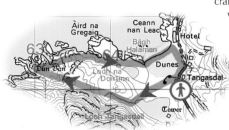

crannog. In early days the tower was thought to have been much taller, possibly three storeys high.

Continuing along the loch shore, a stile and then a small bridge take you to the foot of **Beinn Tangabhal**. The route now strikes west-north-west towards the coast, and marker posts guide you past various archaeological sites. As you proceed, a number of cairns become visible in the distance, and lead to a good vantage point above the shore. To the north there is a fine view over the exquisite sands of Bàgh Halaman, and to the west you catch a first glimpse of Dùn Bàn, magnificently situated on its narrow headland. Further markers take you briefly

Looking north from Dùn Bàn

west to the coast and then back inland to where a stile crosses the fence.

A short walk brings you to **Dùn Bàn** itself (NL 631 004). Built in the Iron Age, the combination of its original fortifications and its commanding position would have made it almost unassailable. Nevertheless, manning this fort in the teeth of a westerly gale would have been an unenviable task! It is amazing to see the blooms of thrift and roseroot thriving in this hostile environment.

After visiting the dun, either head back to the start, or continue on the longer walk up **Beinn Tangabhal** (Walk 4.8). The route back returns to the stile and then follows the marker posts to the cairns. Next, however, instead of returning inland, you continue to track the shoreline, always taking care when passing the numerous steep-sided inlets. There are more markers to direct you, and the way continues round a small bay of rounded cobbles, and on past **Loch na Doirlinn**. ▶

After passing through a gate and some deep marram grass, you may now access the beach of **Bàgh Halaman**. The sands are inviting, but use caution when crossing the burn at NL 644 004. The sand close to the channel may become soft, particularly after heavy rain. If in doubt, return to the grassy machair. After leaving the beach, a short stroll across the flowery sward takes you back to your starting point.

Even if walking alone, you will have plenty of company: in the nesting season oystercatchers and terns will be shadowing your every movement.

WALK 4.8
Dùn Bàn and Beinn Tangabhal

Start/Finish	Beside the phone box at Tangasdal, 3km west of Castlebay (NF 649 001)
Distance	9km; extended walk 11km
Total Ascent	350m; extended walk 500m
Time	4–5hrs; extended walk 6–7hrs
Terrain	Hill and rocky/sandy coast
Maps	OS Explorer 452; OS Landranger 31

This superb outing includes an amazing variety of physical landscapes, as well as sites of historical interest. There is also plenty for the botanist and ornithologist to admire, especially as the walk visits a range of contrasting habitats: machair, moorland, and both rocky and sandy coastlines. The extended walk, adding the cliff scenery of south-west Barra, is strenuous and, for much of the route, unguided. Sound navigational skills are required and also appropriate footwear to negotiate the challenging terrain: steep, rocky slopes interspersed with wet, boggy ground. It is wise to undertake this walk on a clear day, not only to simplify the route finding, but also to enjoy the wonderful views.

If desired, the walk may be shortened at various points. You could return from Dùn Bàn before the ascent of Beinn Tangabhal (Walk 4.7), and it is possible to bypass the cliff section by descending directly back to Dùn Bàn from the top of the Beinn.

Follow the directions for Walk 4.7 as far as Dùn Bàn. These take you close to the foot of **Beinn Tangabhal**.

To ascend the Beinn, first go south from the dun for about 300m to the head of a spectacular inlet (NL 630 002). A narrow ravine trends south from here and leads to the upper slopes of the Beinn. Follow the left-hand edge of this ravine, passing a number of small waterfalls and plunge pools as you climb. In the springtime there is an added bonus; the sheltered, shady confines of this

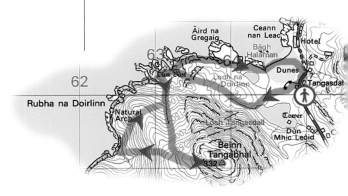

The ravine leading up to Beinn Tangabhal

secluded place are illuminated by wild flowers. Presently, the valley opens out into moorland, with two broad ridges ascending to the summit, one trending in a north-north-westerly direction and the other rising more gently from the west. Although somewhat daunting, the latter option, with its more gradual gradient, is probably the better option.

Head south across heather and grass until you reach the shoulder at NL 634 992. As the ground flattens out, veer east up steeper, rockier terrain. A prominent cairn is soon revealed, as if needed for encouragement, and then the ground levels off, with huge, gently sloping slabs of gneiss affording a natural pavement to the trig point.

The views from the summit of **Beinn Tangabhal** are expansive, but you must abandon the trig point itself to experience the full extent of the panorama: islands, headlands and bays set against the vast backdrop of the Atlantic. Now, another decision: to descend back to the dun, or to continue down to the sea stacks at NL 625 993. Whichever option you choose, first return west from

Stack and cliffs off south-west Barra

the summit, past the prominent cairn, and down once more to the shoulder. To descend from here, the route is relatively straightforward, almost due north for 800m until you meet the upper reaches of the ravine and then down its right flank. In clear weather, the dun is also visible to help guide you down. From the foot of the ravine, either return to the dun once more, or take a short cut, heading north-east for 400m back to the stile at NL 633 003. The route home from there is described in Walk 4.7.

To continue on the extended walk, first head west from the shoulder to where the ground begins to fall away more steeply at NL 630 993. The next target is the clifftop at NL 625 993. Descend carefully over steep, mixed ground until, as you approach the cliffs, the ground levels off. Keep well back from the edge. The sea cliffs appear suddenly and may induce a sense of vertigo. Peering over you see stacks and a cave at NL 624 997, the probable entrance to the arch marked on the OS map. You will undoubtedly be entertained by a variety of sea birds and, in season, the ground is decorated by thrift and other wild flowers.

The route back to the start from here first heads north-east inland from the clifftop to reach the foot of a broad, grassy gully. Now follow this gully up to the col at NL628 998. The climb is a bit of a grind, but as you move over the rise, Barra's superb Atlantic coastline is revealed. Continue, now downwards, still in a north-westerly direction, until you intercept the ravine followed earlier in the day. The ravine takes you back to the dun and the route home.

WALK 4.9

Vatersay (Bhatarsaigh)

Start/Finish	Small car park close to the Annie Jane monument (NL 632 952)
Distance	7km
Total Ascent	100m
Time	3–4hrs
Terrain	Machair and sandy coast
Maps	OS Explorer 452; OS Landranger 31

Vatersay is an extraordinary island, not only in relation to its unique geomorphology, but also on account of its turbulent recent history. After its people were evicted during the Clearances, the island was reclaimed by the Vatersay Raiders: men, mainly from neighbouring Barra and Mingulay, desperate for land. In 1908, after a prolonged legal wrangle and imprisonment of the Raiders, the land was divided into crofts and the island resettled.

The walk described here visits Vatersay's three principal beaches and crosses areas of machair, which, in season, host an extensive variety of flora. The route mainly involves leisurely walking over sand and grass, but some areas may become boggy after a rainy spell. Suitable footwear is recommended. Marker posts are in place along most of the route.

The monument commemorates the 350 people who died when the ship Annie Jane, which had been transporting emigrants to Canada, was wrecked on Bàgh Siar in 1853.

From the car park, walk the short distance across the machair to the obvious **monument** on the edge of the dunes. ◄

From the monument, head south, either across the machair or along the beach beside **Bàgh Siar**. At the end of the beach, a gate gives access back inland. Now, continue towards the **dun**, up steepish ground where, in spring, the grass is adorned with splashes of floral colour. A flatter area below the dun marks the site of a Bronze Age burial cairn excavated in the 1990s.

The dun itself is an excellent viewpoint, particularly looking north over Vatersay's sandy isthmus. However, its defensive credentials have long been eroded. Much of the original stone has been removed to be used in other local building projects.

Leave the dun, heading south-south-east, and descend, passing through a gateway. As you proceed, take care not to antagonise the local cattle. They should be docile enough, but the ground may be rutted and uneven from their trampling.

Continuing the walk in a southerly direction, there are occasional marker posts, but, unfortunately, some seem to have

The standing stone with Mingulay beyond

vanished, perhaps victims of over-enthusiastic live-stock. The next target is a standing stone at NL 628 939. Although its origin is uncertain, it is a useful landmark, and its location near the crest of the rise offers fine views south to Sandray, Pabbay and Mingulay.

After this point, the route changes direction, trending east towards distant **Eòrasdail**, along Vatersay's southern coastline. Markers lead you down to the white sands of **Bàgh a' Deas**. Less frequented than Vatersay's other beaches, it is tranquil and serene, and also favoured by oystercatchers. From the eastern end of the beach, the land rises up gentle, grassy slopes, and, as you climb over the crest of the hill, the view extends down to the ruins of Eòrasdail, a settlement abandoned in the 1970s. The route continues north from here, following the line of an old wall towards the southern shore of **Bàgh Bhatarsaigh** (NL 647 947). This magnificent bay was, in the past, a popular anchorage for The Royal Yacht Britannia.

Now follow the coastline westwards towards the beach. Although the route is less scenic along this stretch,

Bàgh Bhatarsaigh

it remains interesting. The rocky shore is a good place to observe seals and possibly otters. On the approach to the village, you pass an old pier, a reminder of the once prosperous herring industry.

For the final section of the walk, you descend once again to the sand beside the clear, vivid waters of the bay. On a sunny summer's day, it is not difficult to imagine being in a distant tropical paradise!

Stroll slowly north and, about 200m before the end of the beach, turn west over the dunes back to the car park.

WALK 4.10
Mingulay (Miùghlaigh)

Start/Finish	Beach close to the old settlement (NL 566 833)
Distance	6km
Total Ascent	350m
Time	3hrs
Terrain	Hill and rocky coast
Maps	OS Explorer 452; OS Landranger 31

The island of Mingulay, which lies 20km south of Barra, has been uninhabited since the early 20th century. However, the island is truly spectacular and is definitely worth a visit. Mingulay rivals St Kilda for its awesome cliff scenery, but it boasts additional attractions: a beautiful, unspoilt beach, and also the absence of a military presence. The island may be accessed by private boat hired from Barra (see Appendix D) and, on favourable days, as well as going ashore, it may be possible to sail through the arches and geos on the Atlantic side of the island.

This walk combines a visit to the beach and settlement on the more sheltered east coast with a clifftop excursion to the wilder, west side. It is essential to take care at all times and to treat the area with the utmost respect. Rescue from such a remote island, even with a minor injury, would be difficult and potentially hazardous.

The precise start for the walk will depend on where you come ashore, but this is normally at either end of Bagh Mhiùghlaigh. Also, the length of your walk must be tailored to suit your available time on the island.

From the beach, it is worth first visiting the ruined village; in its heyday, almost 200 people lived here. Most of the buildings have long been in a state of decay, but the old schoolhouse near the southern end of the bay has recently been renovated and is used as a bothy.

After exploring the settlement, head inland past the sand dunes, in a north-westerly direction. The land is quite steep and the surface rough, with more widespread heather colonisation since sheep

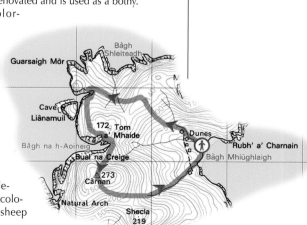

171

Looking towards the old settlement (photo: A Banks)

MACPHEE'S HILL

Cnoc Mhic a' Phì ('MacPhee's hill') is named after a lad from Barra who according to tradition was abandoned on the island. The tale, which may well be based on fact, dates from the 14th century. It is said that after a long break in communication with the people of Mingulay, MacNeil, the clan chief on Barra, became concerned for their wellbeing. A boat was despatched from Barra, and MacPhee was sent ashore to investigate. He found that the whole population of the island had died from disease, and shouted this news back to the boat. Fearing for their health, the crew returned to Barra minus the unfortunate MacPhee. It is said that he survived on shellfish, and meat from the local livestock, and that he used to climb the now legendary hill on northern Mingulay, scanning the horizon in hope of rescue. His fate is uncertain, but one account claims that MacPhee was rescued from this ordeal and was subsequently granted land on Mingulay by MacNeil of Barra.

Liànamuil

were withdrawn from the island. You are aiming for
the broad ridge between **Cnoc Mhic a' Phì** and **Tom a'
Mhaide** (NL 559 838), where you may first glimpse the
western precipices.

The view north is but a taster of what is to come,
looking past the cliffs and sea stacks of Na Gilleacha
Ruadha (the Red Boys) towards Pabbay, Sandray and
Barra. Now head west, aiming for the apex of the narrow
inlet at NL 552 839. It is probably easier to contour round
the slope to avoid losing height. The severity of the drop,
when you near the edge, is literally breathtaking.

The eye is drawn down and across to **Liànamuil** with its gaping cave. There are seabirds everywhere: some teetering precariously on ledges, others hovering over the abyss. In early summer, it is wise to keep a look out for the Great Skua, and be prepared, if necessary, to take evasive action.

Along the northern side of the inlet you gain a view of the narrow vertiginous cleft between **Liànamuil** and the main island. Old accounts suggest that a rope bridge was suspended across this gap to enable sheep to graze the pasture, fertilised by an abundance of guano. ◄

Mingulay and its stacks are a major breeding ground for razorbill, fulmar, guillemot, kittiwake, shag and puffin. As on St Kilda, seabirds formed a significant part of the islanders' diet.

After imbibing the intoxicating atmosphere around Lianamul, head south along the clifftop and over **Tom a' Mhaide** to the head of another inlet, **Bàgh na h-Aoineig** (NL 554 832), beside Mingulay's highest cliff, **Bual na Creige** (Biulacraig), which plummets a vertical 229m to the Atlantic below. A fitting tribute to such an awe-inspiring place, 'Biulacraig' became a rallying cry for the clan MacNeil.

A short distance to the south is **Càrnan** with its trig point, Mingulay's highest point. From there, you look south to Berneray and to Barra Head lighthouse, perched on the southern tip of the Hebridean archipelago. If time permits, continue south-west from the summit to view more awesome rock scenery around Arnamuil, Mingulay's other major stack. Huge igneous dykes may be seen, cross-cutting the ancient gneiss. However, do not linger for too long. For such a small island, it is a surprisingly strenuous walk back to the beach. From Càrnan's summit descend east down steep slopes. After 800m a burn leads east-north-east to the southern end of Bàgh Mhiùghlaigh.

APPENDIX A

Glossary of Gaelic and Norse terms

The following lists contain Gaelic words and Norse suffixes often found in Hebridean place names. It is worth noting that, in certain grammatical situations, some of the Gaelic words add an 'h'. For example, the Gaelic word for little, *beag* becomes *bheag*.

Gaelic	English		
abhainn	river	*garbh*	rough
acarseid	anchorage	*geal*	white
àird	point, headland	*geodha*	chasm
àirigh	shieling	*glas*	grey
allt	burn	*gleann*	glen
bàgh	bay	*gobhar*	goat
baile	town	*iar*	west
bàn	white	*lag*	hollow
beag	little	*leathad*	slope
bealach	pass, saddle	*leathann*	broad
beinn	hill	*liath*	grey
buidhe	yellow	*loch*	lake
cadha	ravine	*machair*	grassy plain
caisteal	castle	*meall*	hill
caladh	harbour	*mòine*	peat
caolas	narrows, sound	*monadh*	moor
ceann	head	*mòr*	big
clach	stone	*mullach*	top
clachan	village	*oitir*	coast
cladach	beach, shore	*rubha*	headland
cleit	ridge	*sgeir*	rock
cnoc	small hill	*sgurr*	mountain
coille	wood	*slochd*	pit
coire	corrie	*sròn*	nose
creag	cliff	*taigh*	house
dearg	red	*tràigh*	shore
deas	south	*tuath*	north
dorcha	dark	*uaimh*	cave
druim	back	*uisge*	water
dubh	black		
each	horse	**Norse**	**English**
ear	east	*-ay*	island
eas	waterfall	*-bhal (val)*	hill
eilean	island	*-bost*	farm
fada	long	*-dal*	valley
fiadh	deer	*-nis*	headland
fraoch	heather	*-vat*	loch, water
		-vig	bay

175

The chasm between Liànamuil and the main island (Walk 4.10)

APPENDIX B

Route summary table

The following table lists the routes, and provides a summary of the estimated walk time, distance, ascent and principal terrain. Generally speaking, the longer walks, in terms of both time and distance, are in the moorland areas, particularly on the east side of North and South Uist.

Walk	Title	Distance (km)	Ascent (m)	Time (hrs)	Terrain
North Uist					
1.1	Berneray	12	200	5–6	Machair; sandy coast
1.2	Udal	8	100	3–4	Machair; sandy coast
1.3	Crògearraidh Mòr	3–4	180–250	2	Hill
1.4	Lochportain	9	250	4–5	Hill; rocky coast
1.5	Li a Tuath and Li a Deas	11–14	300–500	4–7	Hill; moor
1.6	Langais	3.5–6	150	2–3	Hill; moor
1.7	Burabhal	6–12	150–250	3–7	Hill; rocky coast
1.8	Eabhal from Loch Euphort	11–12	350	4–5	Hill; moor
1.9	Eabhal from Cladach Chairinis	12	350	4–5	Hill; moor
1.10	Grimsay	2.5	<50	1–2	Moor

Walk	Title	Distance (km)	Ascent (m)	Time (hrs)	Terrain
1.11	Scolpaig	6	150	3	Hill; rocky coast
1.12	Hogha Gearraidh and Hosta	5	150	2–3	Rocky coast; sandy coast
1.13	Balranald Nature Reserve	7	< 50	3–4	Machair; sandy coast
1.14	Baleshare	7	< 50	3	Sandy coast
Benbecula					
2.1	Borgh	8	< 50	3–4	Machair; sandy coast
2.2	Culla Bay	2.5	< 50	1–2	Sandy coast
2.3	Ròisinis	13	200	5–6	Moor
2.4	Ruabhal	4	120	2	Hill; moor
South Uist					
3.1	Loch Sgioport	5–7	200	3–4	Moor
3.2	Uisinis lighthouse and Nicolson's Leap	17	500	6–8	Moor; rocky coast
3.3	The Northern Corries of Thacla	13	700	5–6	Hill; moor
3.4	The Three Peaks	16–17	1300	5–7	Hill
3.5	Beinn Mhòr from Sniseabhal	10–11	650	4–5	Hill; moor
3.6	Beinn Mhòr from Taobh a Tuath Loch Aineort	10	650	4–5	Hill; moor
3.7	Taobh a Tuath Loch Aineort	4	100	1–2	Hill; moor

Walk	Title	Distance (km)	Ascent (m)	Time (hrs)	Terrain
3.8	Stulaigh	13	800	5–6	Hill; moor
3.9	Gleann Dail bho Dheas	12	400	5–6	Hill; moor
3.10	Eriskay	7	250	3–4	Hill; sandy coast
3.11	Machair Way (Tobha Mòr)	5	< 50	1–2	Machair; sandy coast
3.12	Machair Way (Aisgernis/Cladh Hàlainn)	5	100	2	Machair; sandy coast
Barra					
4.1	Barra's northern peninsula	5–8	150	4–5	Hill; sandy coast
4.2	Cliaid	4.5	220	3	Hill; sandy coast
4.3	Allathasdal	8	200	2–3	Moor; sandy coast
4.4	The Barra Watershed	6	600	3	Hill; moor
4.5	Barra's highest hills	5	400	2–3	Hill
4.6	Central Barra	16	1000	6–8	Hill
4.7	Dùn Bàn	5	100	2–3	Rocky coast; sandy coast
4.8	Dùn Bàn & Beinn Tangabhal	9–11	350–500	4–7	Hill; rocky/sandy coast
4.9	Vatersay	7	100	3–4	Machair; sandy coast
4.10	Mingulay	6	350	3	Hill; rocky coast

APPENDIX C
Further reading

General
The Outer Hebrides by Malcolm MacGregor (Frances Lincoln 2007)

The Scottish Islands by Hamish Haswell-Smith (Canongate 1996)

Uists and Barra by Francis Thompson (David and Charles 2008)

Landscape and wildlife
Machair: Scotland's Living Landscapes by John Love (SNH 2003)

The Highlands and Islands by F. Fraser Darling and J. Morton Boyd (Collins New Naturalist 1969)

The Outer Hebrides: Moor and Machair by Stewart Angus (White Horse Press 2001)

North Uist
North Uist by Erskine Beveridge (Birlinn 2001)

North Uist in History and Legend by Bill Lawson (John Donald 2004)

Benbecula
Benbecula by Ray Burnett (Mingulay 1986)

South Uist
Folklore and Folk Songs of South Uist by Margaret Fay Shaw (Birlinn 2001)

Stories from South Uist by Angus Maclellan (Birlinn 1997)

Barra
Barra and The Bishop's Isles by Keith Branigan and Patrick Foster (NPI Media Group 2002)

'Tales from Barra': The Coddy by John Macpherson (Birlinn 2003)

Neighbouring islands
Mingulay by Ben Buxton (Birlinn 1995)

The Isle of Skye by Terry Marsh (Cicerone 2010)

Walking on Harris and Lewis by Richard Barrett (Cicerone 2010)

Walking on Rum and the Small Isles by Peter Edwards (Cicerone 2012)

APPENDIX D
Useful information

Tourist information offices
www.visithebrides.com

Castlebay (April–October)
Main Street, Castlebay, Isle of Barra HS9 5XD
Tel. 01871 810336

Lochboisdale (April–October)
Pier Road, Lochboisdale, South Uist HS8 5TH
Tel. 01878 700286

Lochmaddy (April–October)
Pier Road, Lochmaddy, Isle of North Uist HS6 5AA
Tel. 01876 500321

Banks
Royal Bank of Scotland, Castlebay, Isle of Barra
Tel. 01871 810281

Bank of Scotland, Balivanich, Isle of Benbecula
Tel. 01870 602096

Bank of Scotland, Lochmaddy, Isle of North Uist
Tel. 01876 500266

Royal Bank of Scotland, Lochboisdale, Isle of South Uist
Tel. 01878 700399

Camping and caravan sites
Barra
Borve Caravan and Campsite, Borve
Tel. 01871 810878

Campbells Campsite, 77 Borve
Tel. 01871 810408

Croft 183, 183 Bolnabodach
Tel. 01871 890373

Croft No 2 Caravan and Campsite, 2 Eoligarry
Tel. 01871 890327

Scurrival Campsite, 3 Eoligarry
Tel. 01871 890292

Benbecula
Shellbay Caravan and Camping Park, Liniclate
Tel. 01870 602447

North Uist
Balranald Caravan and Campsite, Hougharry
Tel. 01876 510304

Moorcroft Holidays Campsite, Carinish
Tel. 01876 580305

South Uist
Gleanndal Campsite, 3 North Glendale
Tel. 01878 700545

Kilbride Campsite, Cille Bhrighde
Tel. 01878 700568

Hostels and bunkhouses
Barra
Dunard Hostel, Castlebay
Tel. 01871 810443

Benbecula
Nunton House Hostel, Nunton
Tel. 01870 602017

North Uist and Berneray
Berneray Youth Hostel, Isle of Berneray, North Uist
Tel. 0845 293 7373

Taigh Mo Sheanair, Carnach, Claddach Baleshare, Isle of North Uist
Tel. 01876 580246

South Uist
Howmore Hostel, Howmore
Tel. 0845 293 7373

Uist Bunkhouse, Daliburgh
Tel. 01878 700566

Garages, car hire and breakdown recovery
Creagorry Motors, Creagorry, Isle of Benbecula
Tel. 01870 602838

Maclennan Brothers, Balivanich, Isle of Benbecula
Tel. 01870 602191

Petrol
Castlebay (Barra)
Daliburgh, Lochboisdale (South Uist)
Balivanich, Creagorry (Benbecula)
Bayhead, Lochmaddy (North Uist)

Boat hire
Barra Fishing Charters, Castlebay
Tel. 01871 890384

Cycle hire
Barra Cycle Hire
Tel. 01871 810284

Morrison Cycle Hire, Carinish, North Uist
Tel. 01876 580211

Rothan Cycles, Howmore, South Uist
Tel. 01870 620283

Public transport
Details of bus services on the Uists and Barra are available from:

Comhairle nan Eilean Siar
Tel. 0845 600 7090
www.cne-siar.gov.uk

Medical and emergency services
Hospital
Uist and Barra Hospital, Balivanich, Isle of Benbecula
Tel. 01870 603603

Doctors
Barra Medical Practice, Castlebay, Isle of Barra
Tel. 01871 810282

Benbecula Medical Practice, Griminish, Isle of Benbecula
Tel. 01870 602215

North Uist Medical Practice, Lochmaddy, Isle of North Uist
Tel. 01876 500333

South Uist Medical, Daliburgh, South Uist
Tel. 01878 700302

Police and mountain rescue
Ring 999, or
Police (01851 702222) or
Coastguard (01851 702013)

Cafés
Hotels available from tourist information offices.

Barra
Airport Café
Ardmhor Café
Bizzee Bee Café
Kisimul Café
The Deck
The Heritage Café (Castlebay)

Benbecula
Airport Café
An Caladh (East Camp Tues–Fri)
Stepping Stone (Balivanich)
Sgoil Lionacleit

Berneray
Lobster Pot Tea-room

Eriskay
Am Politician

North Uist
Taigh Chearsabhagh (Lochmaddy)
Claddach Kirkibost Centre

South Uist
Askernish Golf Club
Hebridean Jewellery (Lochdar)
Kildonan Café (Kildonan Museum)
Lochboisdale Post Office Café
Mary's Café (Carnan)

NOTES

NOTES

LISTING OF CICERONE GUIDES

ITALY

Italy's Sibillini National Park
Shorter Walks in the Dolomites
Ski Touring and Snowshoeing in
  the Dolomites
The Way of St Francis
Through the Italian Alps
Trekking in the Apennines
Trekking in the Dolomites
Via Ferratas of the Italian
  Dolomites: Vol 1
Via Ferratas of the Italian
  Dolomites: Vol 2
Walking and Trekking in the
  Gran Paradiso
Walking in Abruzzo
Walking in Italy's Stelvio
  National Park
Walking in Sardinia
Walking in Sicily
Walking in the Dolomites
Walking in Tuscany
Walking in Umbria
Walking on the Amalfi Coast
Walking the Italian Lakes
Walks and Treks in the
  Maritime Alps

BELGIUM AND LUXEMBOURG

The GR5 Trail – Benelux and
  Lorraine
Walking in the Ardennes

SCANDINAVIA

Walking in Norway

EASTERN EUROPE AND THE BALKANS

The Danube Cycleway Volume 2
The High Tatras
The Mountains of Romania
Walking in Bulgaria's
  National Parks
Walking in Hungary
Mountain Biking in Slovenia
The Islands of Croatia
The Julian Alps of Slovenia
The Mountains of Montenegro
The Peaks of the Balkans Trail
Trekking in Slovenia
Walking in Croatia
Walking in Slovenia:
  The Karavanke

SPAIN AND PORTUGAL

Coastal Walks in Andalucia
Cycle Touring in Spain
Mountain Walking in Mallorca
Mountain Walking in
  Southern Catalunya

Spain's Sendero Histórico: The GR1
The Andalucian Coast to
  Coast Walk
The Mountains of Nerja
The Mountains of Ronda
  and Grazalema
The Northern Caminos
The Sierras of Extremadura
Trekking in Mallorca
Walking and Trekking in the
  Sierra Nevada
Walking in Andalucia
Walking in Menorca
Walking in the Cordillera
  Cantabrica
Walking on Gran Canaria
Walking on La Gomera and
  El Hierro
Walking on La Palma
Walking on Lanzarote and
  Fuerteventura
Walking on Tenerife
Walking on the Costa Blanca
The Camino Portugués
Walking in Portugal
Walking in the Algarve
Walking on Madeira

GREECE, CYPRUS AND MALTA

The High Mountains of Crete
Trekking in Greece
Walking and Trekking on Corfu
Walking in Cyprus
Walking on Malta

INTERNATIONAL CHALLENGES, COLLECTIONS AND ACTIVITIES

Canyoning in the Alps
Europe's High Points
The Via Francigena
  Canterbury to Rome – Part 2

AFRICA

Climbing in the Moroccan
  Anti-Atlas
Mountaineering in the Moroccan
  High Atlas
The High Atlas
Trekking in the Atlas Mountains
Walks and Scrambles in the
  Moroccan Anti-Atlas
Kilimanjaro
Walking in the Drakensberg

TAJIKISTAN

Trekking in Tajikistan

JORDAN

Jordan – Walks, Treks, Caves,
  Climbs and Canyons
Treks and Climbs in Wadi Rum,
  Jordan

ASIA

Annapurna
Everest: A Trekker's Guide
Trekking in the Himalaya
Trekking in Bhutan
Trekking in Ladakh
The Mount Kailash Trek

NORTH AMERICA

British Columbia
The John Muir Trail
The Pacific Crest Trail

SOUTH AMERICA

Aconcagua and the Southern Andes
Hiking and Biking Peru's Inca Trails
Torres del Paine

TECHNIQUES

Fastpacking
Geocaching in the UK
Indoor Climbing
Lightweight Camping
Map and Compass
Outdoor Photography
Polar Exploration
Rock Climbing
Sport Climbing
The Mountain Hut Book

MINI GUIDES

Alpine Flowers
Avalanche!
Navigation
Pocket First Aid and Wilderness
  Medicine
Snow

MOUNTAIN LITERATURE

8000 metres
A Walk in the Clouds
Abode of the Gods
Fifty Years of Adventure
The Pennine Way – the Path,
  the People, the Journey
Unjustifiable Risk?

For full information on all our
guides, books and eBooks,
visit our website:
www.cicerone.co.uk

Walking – Trekking – Mountaineering – Climbing – Cycling

Over 40 years, Cicerone have built up an outstanding collection of over 300 guides, inspiring all sorts of amazing adventures.

Every guide comes from extensive exploration and research by our expert authors, all with a passion for their subjects. They are frequently praised, endorsed and used by clubs, instructors and outdoor organisations.

All our titles can now be bought as **e-books**, **ePubs** and **Kindle** files and we also have an online magazine – **Cicerone Extra** – with features to help cyclists, climbers, walkers and trekkers choose their next adventure, at home or abroad.

Our website shows any **new information** we've had in since a book was published. Please do let us know if you find anything has changed, so that we can publish the latest details. On our **website** you'll also find great ideas and lots of detailed information about what's inside every guide and you can buy **individual routes** from many of them online.

It's easy to keep in touch with what's going on at Cicerone by getting our monthly **free e-newsletter**, which is full of offers, competitions, up-to-date information and topical articles. You can subscribe on our home page and also follow us on **Facebook** and **Twitter** or dip into our **blog**.

Cicerone – the very best guides for exploring the world.

CICERONE

Juniper House, Murley Moss, Oxenholme Road, Kendal, Cumbria LA9 7RL
Tel: 015395 62069 info@cicerone.co.uk
www.cicerone.co.uk